WHEN
FOOD'S
A FOE

**Books by Nancy J. Kolodny
and Robert C. Kolodny**

*How to Survive Your
  Adolescent's Adolescence*

Smart Choices

WHEN FOOD'S A FOE

How to Confront and Conquer Eating Disorders

REVISED & UPDATED

NANCY J. KOLODNY, M.A., M.S.W.

 LITTLE, BROWN AND COMPANY

Boston   Toronto   London

Revised Edition

The author is grateful to the following for permission to use previously published material:

"The Eating Attitudes Test: An Index of the Symptoms of Anorexia Nervosa," by D. M. Garner and P. E. Garfinkel, *Psychological Medicine*, 9 (1979): 278.

Excerpts from Boston Children's Hospital with S. Baker & R. Henry, *Parents' Guide to Nutrition*, © 1986, Addison-Wesley Publishing Company, Inc., Reading, Massachusetts. Pp. 43, 128, 129 & 166. Reprinted with permission.

Tables from "Fast Foods 1986: Nutrient Analysis," reprinted with permission of Ross Laboratories, Columbus, OH 43216, from *Dietetic Currents*, v. 13, no. 6, copyright © 1986 Ross Laboratories.

"Cathy" cartoons by Cathy Guisewite. Copyright © 1985, 1986 by Universal Press Syndicate. Reprinted with permission. All rights reserved.

"Bloom County" cartoon by Berke Breathed. Copyright © 1986, The Washington Post Writers Group. Reprinted with permission.

Definitions from the DSM III-R: American Psychiatric Association, *Diagnostic and Statistical Manual of Mental Disorders, Third Edition, Revised*. Washington, D.C.: American Psychiatric Association, 1987.

M. C. Smith and M. H. Thelen, "Development and Validation of a Test for Bulimia," *Journal of Consulting and Clinical Psychology*, 52 (1984): 863–72. Copyright © 1992 by the American Psychological Association. Reprinted by permission.

Library of Congress Cataloging-in-Publication Data
Kolodny, Nancy J.
    When food's a foe : how to confront and conquer eating disorders / Nancy J. Kolodny. — Rev. ed.
        p.   cm.
    Includes bibliographical references.
    Summary: Examines the causes and effects of bulimia and anorexia and discusses ways in which these disorders can be prevented.
    ISBN 0-316-50181-6
    1. Eating disorders — Juvenile literature.   2. Anorexia nervosa — Juvenile literature.   3. Bulimia — Juvenile literature.   [1. Eating disorders.   2. Anorexia nervosa.   3. Bulimia.]   I. Title.
RC552.E18K65 1992
616.85'26 — dc20   91-37304
                        10 9 8 7 6 5 4 3 2 1
                                RRD–VA

*Published simultaneously in Canada
by Little, Brown & Company (Canada) Limited*

Printed in the United States of America

This book is dedicated with love to my husband, Robert, our daughters, Linda, Lora, and Lisa, and with gratitude to the many people struggling with eating disorders who have allowed me to work with them and learn from them.

An Invitation to the Readers of
WHEN FOOD'S A FOE

If you have a question about anything discussed in this book, or a suggestion about any subject I should have included but didn't, or if you would just like to send your comments, I'd really like to hear from you. Write

Nancy J. Kolodny
c/o Little, Brown and Company
34 Beacon Street
Boston, MA 02108

CONTENTS

INTRODUCTION

Most of us take food and eating for granted. We all have preferences for certain kinds of foods at one time or another, we know what it means to be hungry and how it feels to satisfy hunger, and we also know that the act of eating involves more than just meeting the nutritional needs of our bodies. Eating plays a very important role in our social lives and is often a kind of recreation, or even a sport that we share with people we like.

Recently, though, a problem has grown up around food and eating. People — mostly teenagers and young adults — have developed eating disorders. These disorders upset the whole set of behaviors that come so easily to most of us when it's mealtime — sitting down, eating what's served or choosing what to serve and then eating it, and enjoying the experience — and turn the process into something else. Mealtimes become occasions for conflict, extreme distress, and even physical discomfort. The dining table becomes a battleground, where wars are fought between people and even within individuals themselves.

What happens when people develop eating disorders? They don't think about food or use food the way the majority of people do. Instead of eating when they're hungry, eating for nutrition and good health, eating for pleasure, or eating to share good times with others, they get into bizarre relationships with food and do things that aren't considered "normal" — such as developing odd rituals before they allow themselves to eat, or needing to immediately rid their bodies of the food they've eaten by self-induced or emetic-induced vomiting (an emetic is a medication that makes you throw up) or taking laxatives to purge their systems. They're likely to become so obsessed with food that eating or not eating become physically and emotionally destructive, almost like dealing with an addiction: the more it's done and the longer it's done, the stronger is its hold and the harder it is to kick. As the focus on food and eating dominates their daily routines, their families and friends get caught up with them on an emotional roller coaster that is hard for everyone to cope with and even harder to understand. If they can't get themselves out of this self-destructive cycle and don't get help to break the hold the eating disorder has on them, the result can be physical damage (sometimes irreversible), as well as emotional problems, such as depression. Some people even become suicidal when they're unable to cope with the sense of loss of control and poor self-esteem that an eating disorder can cause. *Eating disorders can kill.*

What are these disorders? There are two that are on the upswing among teenagers and young adults today — anorexia nervosa and bulimia. Anorexia nervosa is a self-starvation disorder in which the anorectic (the person afflicted with anorexia) ignores hunger, restricts the amounts and kinds of food eaten to such an extent that starvation (with all its debilitating effects) is a very real possibility — *as is death.* Bulimia is a binge-purge behavior that compels the bulimic (the person afflicted with bulimia) to gorge (binge) on enormous amounts of food (sometimes many thousands of calories at one time) and then get rid of it (purge) by means of vomiting or excessive use of laxatives. It is just as dangerous to one's physical and mental health as anorexia is, though the physical side effects are different. Some people who struggle with these eating disorders are anorectic part of the time and bulimic part of the time, never quite escaping the vicious circle that entraps them. Females are victims more often than males but, increasingly, young men are showing up for counseling. And people from all walks of life, all ethnic and socioeconomic groups are vulnerable. Eating disorders can touch you whether you live on a farm or on Fifth Avenue, in a ghetto or in a mansion, or anywhere in between.

How do these disorders start? Believe it or not, there's an illogical logic to eating disorders. For some people they can actually serve a purpose — providing a focus to an otherwise frustrating or unhappy existence, a specific way of coping with problems that can't be openly discussed, confronted, or handled in any other fashion, a substitute for self-esteem. An eating disorder is a red flag, telling you that you need to pay attention to some situation in your life that you're ignoring or avoiding. An eating disorder is a reminder that you aren't giving voice to whatever stresses and frustrations you may be experiencing. The bottom line is that eating disorders are a self-destructive way of making a statement about dissatisfaction with the way things are going in one's life. People don't usually *consciously* choose to do this to themselves at the outset, however. One wouldn't say, "I think I'll become an anorectic to show everyone just how cool I really am and how in control I can be" or "I think I'll become a bulimic because it's such fun to overeat and I'll show everyone I can do as I please and not suffer any consequences."

Sometimes eating disorders can be triggered when they start out as innocent attempts to be part of a crowd. This is particularly true of bulimia, which may begin as a weekend ritual of living it up with friends by pigging out and then getting rid of the food by purging, because all of the participants are operating on the incorrect assumption that this will prevent weight gain. Bulimia has become a serious health problem on many college campuses where weekends are reserved for letting off steam and indulging oneself after sweating it out over the books for five days solid. In susceptible people, anorexia can be triggered by wanting to be "in" with friends who are dieting as a group to achieve a certain goal (for example, to look good in swimsuits on the beach in the summer) or dieting to fit the thin image our society tells us makes people more desirable. The problems begin when it's time to stop either the dieting or the bingeing and purging. Some people just can't and won't. The reasons for this are complicated and will be discussed all through this book. But whatever the reasons people have for becoming anorectic or bulimic, the end results can be disastrous to both physical and mental health, to family harmony, to friendships and romantic relationships, and to school or work performance.

An eating disorder doesn't just pop up out of nowhere. It's a symptom, a signal that something is wrong in a person's life. Unfortunately, defining and correcting an eating disorder isn't as straightforward as diagnosing a medical condition like measles or chicken pox, where a doctor knows exactly what the cause is, how you catch it, how long the illness will last, and what the best course of treatment is. People who are susceptible to developing eating disorders may have similar kinds of family histories, may share certain personality traits with other anorectics and bulimics, and their symptoms can be described, but treating and curing these disorders isn't easy and there are no immunizations available to protect people from getting anorexia or bulimia. We can't impose a cure and make someone with an eating disorder get well by offering a pill or a shot. Someone suffering from anorexia or bulimia has to be willing to get well and must put forth a lot of effort to help that process occur. It's an interesting, challenging process that's sometimes humorous, sometimes poignant and even painful; it's a process that's worth the effort because it can help you learn so much about yourself.

Although it isn't easy to cure eating disorders, it *is* possible to prevent them. The best prevention is knowing the facts about eating disorders to avoid being trapped in their maze in the first place, or learning the facts even if you're trapped, so that you'll fully understand what you're doing and what your options are.

Giving you this information and showing you what to do with it is the purpose of *When Food's a Foe*. If you're a victim of an eating disorder yourself, if you think you could be, or if you're a relative, friend, or coworker of someone who has anorexia or bulimia, this book will help you recognize and define the symptoms, acknowledge the problem, learn what you can and can't do to help yourself or someone else, and learn specific strategies that can ease your way out of the situation. *When Food's a Foe* is a book for you to work with, a portable confidant that will hear you out and offer sound advice. It's a book that will challenge you to think, ask you to do some work, and help you learn to honestly face yourself and the people you care about. It's designed to give you back some of the control you may feel is missing in your life, and to help you make choices for constructive change that will make it possible for you or someone you know to let go of an eating disorder bit by bit.

Try to read *When Food's a Foe* from the Introduction through to the last chapter in numerical order, without skipping around, because each chapter builds on the information offered in the previous one. The book is designed to give you a clear and complete picture of eating disorders and should help you unravel the gradual process that takes someone from habits to obsessions, master the things that can be done to reverse that process, and learn ways to maintain enough control to be able to stay away from the abnormal end of eating behaviors.

If you have anorexia or bulimia already, and if you read the information, do the exercises, and try out some of the suggestions in this book, *When Food's a Foe* will help you make the positive commitment to yourself that you'll need to conquer your eating disorder. If you're a parent, friend, or in any other kind of relationship with an anorectic or bulimic, reading *When Food's a Foe* should help you understand better what someone with an eating disorder has to contend with, how you fit into his or her struggle, and how you can voice your concerns and frustrations without making the problem worse. If you believe you might be on the verge of developing anorexia or bulimia, *When Food's a Foe* can help you short-circuit your present system of attitudes, beliefs, and communication and install one that functions better and that will give you a fighting chance to prevent an eating disorder from creeping into your life.

PART 1

EATING DISORDERS EXPLAINED

1
WHEN YOU LOOK
IN THE MIRROR

Self-Image, Body-Image, and the Struggle for Self-Esteem

I found out I was voted "prettiest" the day we got our senior yearbooks. When I looked at my photo on that page, all I could focus on was that my nose was too broad, my lips uneven, and one of my eyebrows was thicker than the other. I didn't feel like I deserved the vote.

Amy J., age seventeen

Have you ever felt like you're a "perfect 10"? Have you ever said, "I'm honestly satisfied with who I am"? Do you *really* like yourself? Do you give yourself the proverbial "credit where credit is due"? If you have and do, your self-image (your sense of identity) is probably secure, your self-esteem (the positive feelings you have about yourself) is high, and your body-image (what you see when you look in the mirror and how comfortable or satisfied you are about your size, shape, and appearance) is one you're at ease with.

A lot of people, though, can't answer "yes" to any of those questions because they don't accept themselves as they are and barely like themselves at all. Some think that they're losers, that they're worthless, and that if anything good happens to them it's probably just a result of luck. For many others, it's largely because they've bought into a "thin is in/ trim is in" mentality, which is based on a myth that how a person looks and how little he or she weighs is of *primary* importance, and this mentality dominates their lives.

We happen to live in a weight-conscious, fashion-conscious, diet-conscious society that puts a premium on good looks, isn't very tolerant of physical imperfection, and sends out a message suggesting that people who are thin and trim are somehow smarter, luckier, more interesting than, and generally superior to, those who aren't. So it's not exactly unreasonable that someone would want to be thin. But to focus too much energy trying to achieve that elusive look can be physically and psychologically draining, making it very hard to accomplish much else — such as learning about ourselves, exploring and developing skills and talents, getting to know other people, and forming emotional attachments.

What exactly are self-image, body-image, self-perception, and self-esteem, and how are they connected? How can you tell if you're having problems in any of these areas and might be headed in the direction of developing an eating disorder? Read on.

Chain Links

Self-Image: What is self-image? It's your sense of who you are and who you want to become, your identity. Self-image can change frequently because of all the outside influences and pressures that shape it: your parents' hopes and expectations for you, the values and beliefs you have, the impact of friends' opinions, the things you learn in school and what you learn about yourself as you progress through school, jobs you may have, fads and fashions, people you admire, and so on, and it can take a while for you to develop a self-image that you're happy with. Until you do you're susceptible to a lot of emotional ups and downs because you're reacting to these influences and pressures, making adjustments, and trying to find a comfortable match between the external pressures and expectations and your own private ones.

Body-Image: A big part of self-image is tied to body-image — how comfortable or satisfied a person feels about his or her size, shape, and appearance. Body-image is changeable too, and it has some peculiar characteristics:

- what you see when you look in a mirror or think about yourself (little flaws, big flaws, imperfections) may be different from what others see when they look at you (someone else may think you look absolutely perfect);
- what you think you see may not be there (anorectics, for example, see fat on their bodies where none exists);
- if you're feeling happy, your body-image may seem just fine to you; if you're sad or down, you may feel like there's nothing right about the image you're seeing in the mirror (this change can happen in a matter of minutes);
- there's usually an ideal body-image (how you'd look if you could make yourself "perfect") you carry around in the back of your mind, and it often clashes with the reality of what you see in the mirror. 189

How do you develop an ideal body-image? Most of us pay attention to the "three P's" — parents, peers, and the press. From these sources you can take what you like and disregard what you don't, and turn what's left into your personal, ideal body-image. Maybe a guy wants to look like Billy Idol, M. C. Hammer, or Bo Jackson, or a girl imagines herself looking like Whitney Houston, Mariah Carey, or her own mom. Usually, you'll incorporate a bit of this look and a bit of that one to come up with something unique — a look that feels right for you, that captures the essence of who you are that moment.

Whatever you're aiming for, having an ideal body-image can be useful. It's more than just wanting to be in style, more than silly fantasy — it's a way to define yourself, a visual shorthand that lets other people look at you and make some accurate assumptions about the kind of person you are. It's a way to try to get status and connect with certain people. For example, when you're a teenager, being part of a crowd is important, and if the kids in your crowd put down people who are on the minus side of being physically attractive (however they define "attractive"), you'll try hard not to be like those people. If being thin is an important part of your friends' values, you'll probably accept that value as your own. Unfortunately, some people aren't built to be thin, and for them, trying to get thin can be a real problem.

Self-Esteem and Self-Perception: If you can't look the way you think you're supposed to, no matter how hard you try or want to, your ideal and actual body-images clash and you become very vulnerable to self-doubts and feelings of inadequacy. Your self-esteem (the good feelings you have about yourself) may suffer and your self-perception (how you rate yourself, how you think you're coming across to other people, how you interpret their reactions to you) may be off base and not reflect what's actually going on.

Why Is THIN So Important?

In our society the press — on TV and radio, in newspapers and magazines as well as the movie industry — have promoted the notion that physical perfection is important and that our appearance somehow defines the kind of person each of us is. Female physical perfection is shown as a thin, agile body on which clothes look fashion-magazine perfect (for men, the desirable "look" is more varied, ranging from Rambos to runners, all of whom are muscular and obviously fit), and the message for women is that the potential for happiness, popularity, or success relates to how little they weigh. Here's a glaring example of this bias, which occurred during the March 16, 1990, 5:30 p.m. news on WTNH-TV in Connecticut. Figure skating champions Natalie and Wayne Seybold were being interviewed about their upcoming performance with the Ice Capades. The very first words out of the male interviewer's mouth were, "I read your bios out loud in the newsroom. Ninety-eight pounds! Is that true, Natalie? Do you weigh ninety-eight pounds?" The remark made it seem as if her low weight was what distinguished her from everyone else, that it overshadowed all of her other attributes and achievements.

Here's another example. The October 30, 1990, issue of *Soap Opera Digest* featured a story (illustrated with several photos) about *Days of Our Lives* actress Camilla Scott. The caption beneath one picture of her with a date at a high school formal said, "Even though she was a chubby teen, Camilla still had a social life" (p. 28). Think about the implication that it's unusual for a heavy person to have a social life. Is that fair? Do you buy into that belief system?

Now take a moment to consider the message suggested by this very brief commercial for Slim Fast, a powdered nutritional supplement meant to replace two meals a day for dieters: "It's a way of life — losing weight and feeling great — the Slim Fast way of life." If you think about that logically, you'll end up asking yourself, "Do I really want to be focused on my weight as my *way of life?*" And who says that a dieter's way of life is the normal, desirable one? The diet industry, that's who. According to an article by Carrie White in the February 14, 1991, edition of the *Palm Beach Post* people in the United States spend thirty-two billion dollars — yes, that's *billion* — daily on weight loss products such as diet sodas, diet foods, and health club memberships in pursuit of that ideal (but elusive) body-image.

Interestingly, the men and women who represent these ideal images we revere don't look the same in real life, but we tend to forget that when we try to imitate them. Consider body builder and movie star Arnold Schwarzenegger, for example. Seen at poolside at a Las Vegas hotel, he

How Do You See Yourself?

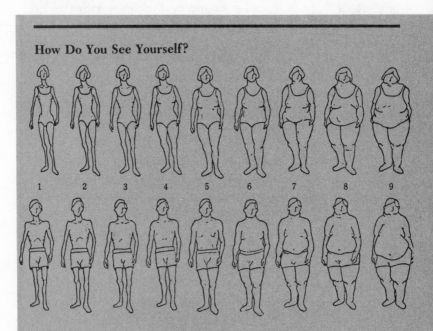

Look at the people above. Then, without thinking about it too much, pick the body that you think:

— Is closest to what you look like.
— Is closest to how you *want* to look.
— Is the body type that's most attractive to the opposite sex.

was inconspicuous and his body — while attractive — was unremarkable. He didn't look like his portrayal of Conan the Barbarian; since he hadn't bothered to slather himself with oil or pump up his muscles before coming outside, he looked more like his character in *Kindergarten Cop*. Likewise, Sylvester Stallone, star of the "Rocky" movies and *Rambo,* is actually around 5'9", although in his movies the camera angles are carefully chosen to make him look taller. Now think about

At the University of Pennsylvania, psychologists Paul Rozin and April Fallon tried this test on college students. The students' answers showed that men and women view their own bodies in dramatically different ways.

Men are satisfied with their looks. The average man says his ideal is body number 4 — that's what he'd like to weigh — and he thinks he actually looks like that. He also thinks women are most attracted to that type — though *women* say they like their men leaner.

College women, in contrast, think pounds of fat lie between them and their ideal. They think, on the average, that their bodies are somewhat slimmer than woman number 4. But they think men would be most attracted to a number 3 body (when men actually say they like women a little *plumper* than that). And finally, these women want to be *even thinner* than that number 3 standard — significantly thinner than they think would be attractive to men.

— *Joel Gurin*

(Source: A. Stukard, T. Sorensen, and F. Schulsinger, "Use of the Danish Adoption Register for the Study of Obesity and Thinness," in *The Genetics of Neurological and Psychiatric Disorders,* edited by S. Kety, 119. New York: Raven Press, 1980. Copyright © 1983 by Raven Press, New York. Used by permission.)

fashion models. If you've ever seen a "before and after" make-over in a magazine you know how much of a role illusion plays in the whole beauty business. For most of us, even the media stars, there's quite a gap between ideal and real body-images.

Are You Sowing the Seeds of an Eating Disorder?

Are You Unhappy with Your Body-Image? If you're dissatisfied with your body-image, your total self-image will suffer. You won't exactly be loaded with self-esteem. When you don't have self-esteem it's hard to give yourself credit for much, and so your self-perception will be affected. It may go down a notch or two and you may begin to think of yourself as a loser or a fake when someone more objective would say that's not so.

> I've always wanted to be popular. I don't enjoy being known as a brain, but my mind is so much better than my looks. I'm shy normally, so I find it hard to make friends. I know if I were thinner people would like me more; at least they'd take a look at me and see I fit the image of the in group up here. Then maybe they'd forget that my SAT scores led the school. The way I look right now, I don't think I'd want to be my friend if I were someone else. I'm going on a strict diet today.
>
> *Jeri P., age seventeen*

I can't tell you how many times Jeri and I have discussed what she just said to you. None of us put her down for being smart; she just can't give herself credit for it. She never believes us when we congratulate her for things like awards she gets at school. She thinks we're making fun. She's never happy with herself. And she has a few really *good* friends. I know a lot of girls with a zillion acquaintances and no friends they can really trust. I wish Jeri could realize there's a difference between friends for show and friends for real. I'm worried about her.

> *Nancy D., age seventeen,*
> *Jeri's best friend*

Do You Lack Self-Esteem? Jeri is a perfect example of someone who sees herself one way while other people see her differently. Her intelligence doesn't seem to give her good feelings or enhance her self-esteem. Jeri undervalues herself so much that she says if she were another person she wouldn't want to be her friend, and thinks being thin — changing her physical self — will make everyone like her or at least give her a better chance to make friends. She devalues her best talents and accomplishments and emphasizes the negatives, her shyness and weight.

Is Your Self-Perception Off? Nancy's opinion of Jeri would seem to suggest that Jeri's self-perception isn't close to being accurate. Nancy makes it clear that Jeri not only has friends, but they're the kind of friends other kids would love to have: trustworthy confidants. She also says that the kids in school *do* give Jeri points for being intelligent. Jeri is the one who puts herself down for that.

What's going on, then? Jeri's self-image is distorted and leaves no room for self-esteem. She's unhappy with her body-image, overemphasizing her physical shortcomings. She underrates her emotional and intellectual strengths. She has bought into the cultural "thin is in/trim is in" bias, so the solution she dreams up for changing her life is dieting and getting thin. (Dieting, however, won't address the question of why she can't give herself credit or take credit for the other great things about herself.) Jeri's self-perception is distorted and at odds with what her peers say they really feel about her. It's as if she's wearing an invisible radio headset locked into a frequency that constantly transmits negative messages directly to her brain while it scrambles and obscures anything positive that she might be able to hear, think, or feel about herself.

Jeri and people like her are vulnerable to getting trapped in the eating-disorder maze — developing anorexia nervosa and/or bulimia. There are some real differences between how people who are vulnerable and how those who are relatively immune perceive themselves and live their lives. Are you immune or at risk? Read on.

Your Body-Image: Like It or Loathe It?

The physical changes you go through when you're a teenager are major ones. Growing into an adult body can be exciting, but it can also be frustrating, since you're never quite sure what the end result will be! This process can be further complicated if you don't have accurate information about predictable physical changes during adolescence (girls, for example, increase their percentage of body fat while guys decrease theirs). So, having difficulty accepting your physical self, having problems accepting a discrepancy between your ideal body-image and the real one, and being misinformed or underinformed about the physical side of life during the teen years are some of the factors that can put you at risk of developing an eating disorder. For example, if

- you buy into the "thin is in/trim is in" mentality and attempt to achieve that image at all costs,
- your body-image is frequently a major source of disappointment to you,
- you look in the mirror and usually wish you were someone else,
- you negate compliments about your looks and make it seem like you're not worthy of them,

CATHY
COPYRIGHT 1986 UNIVERSAL PRESS SYNDICATE.

you're a prime candidate for becoming anorectic or bulimic. On the other hand, if

– you're usually realistic about your physical appearance and accept how you look without feeling disappointed in yourself,

    – you try to achieve a look that feels right for you even if it's not the "in" look,

    – you can accept compliments about your looks,

you're probably not at risk.

    Now do the following exercise. It's called "When I Look in the Mirror" and it's designed to get you to react on a gut level. Complete the following half-sentences. It's important that you write the first things that pop into your mind, that you're honest, and that you don't skip anything. Keep writing until all the thoughts you have are down on paper.

    (A reminder: save what you write as you work your way through *When Food's a Foe*. Your responses can help you uncover your concerns and pinpoint areas you may need some professional help coping with.)

When I Look in the Mirror

1. When I look in the mirror, I _____

2. Today I looked in the mirror and _____

3. I like myself best when _____

4. The first thing I do when I get up in the morning is ____
   _____

5. The first thing I think when I get up in the morning is
   _____

6. I feel glad to be me when _____

7. If my mirror could talk, it would say _____

8. My perfect reflection would be _____

9. The last time I liked what I saw in the mirror _____

_____

10. My body is _____

How did it feel to do this exercise? It can be both hard and scary to think about yourself in this way. But it's better to be scared than to keep your feelings bottled up inside you and hidden so that you're not sure what's making you tick. When you don't know what you're dealing with, you can't know how to handle it. If you can define what's bothering you, you have a better shot at fixing it. "When I Look in the Mirror" can help you start the process.

For example, are your answers filled with negative statements about yourself like the following answers taken from people who were in treatment for anorexia and bulimia?

- "My body is gross and keeps me from being my best."
- "If my mirror could talk, it would say, 'You're hopeless.' "
- "I like myself best when I'm under 90 pounds."
- "The last time I liked what I saw in the mirror was never."
- "The first thing I do when I get up in the morning is weigh myself."
- "The first thing I think when I get up in the morning is 'Who will I have to fool today?' "

If your answers have a "downer" feel to them, if they indicate you're really harping on weight, if your body-image is obviously distorted (for example, you *really* see yourself as fat when you're 5'8" and weigh 110 pounds), these are clues that you're taking the first steps toward developing an eating disorder.

Your Intellectual Side:
A Source of Pride or to Be Denied?

People at risk for developing anorexia nervosa and/or bulimia

- don't often give themselves credit for the things they're good at;
- question how useful or valuable their ideas and opinions could be to someone else or to a group;
- feel misunderstood or ignored;
- fall into the habit of thinking and believing that they're never good enough or smart enough, or if they're smart enough, that's not good enough.

> I've always been embarrassed at being able to come in first at so many things I do in school. I feel like I should give others a chance to be first. I feel like a fraud a lot of the time because I'm not that much smarter or better than most of the other kids. I can't remember ever feeling 100 percent happy with myself or proud of myself.
>
> *Sharyn H., age seventeen*

On the other hand, people who are reasonably immune tend to be open to experience and usually

- feel they're capable individuals with something to offer the people in their lives;
- believe they have valid ideas and what they have to say will enhance a discussion;
- feel other people actually listen to them and pay attention to what's being said;
- feel "marketable," with a good chance of being hired for a job or of being given a position of responsibility in school;

– aren't as frightened of failure, so they can take more chances trying new things, even if it means they won't be number one at them.

I entered the local music talent search on a dare. My boy-friend thought I had a shot at it, and that was good enough for me. I figured I had nothing to lose except the time it took to prepare my dress and the concerto I was going to play. It was fun even though there were times when the music just wouldn't flow from my brain to my fingers. All my friends got into helping me rehearse, and came down to the pageant with me. I placed fifth in the state. Well, maybe next year . . .

Arlene De C., age sixteen

Self-Esteem — Just a Dream?

Self-esteem can be hard to come by during adolescence, when emotions tend to swing from highs to lows under the best of circumstances. People who don't have self-esteem usually have difficulty expressing and acknowledging feelings, which puts them at risk of developing eating disorders. For example,

– they keep their emotions under wraps;
– they doubt the validity of the emotions they're experiencing;
– they may even question their right to have such feelings;
– they're afraid to have feelings;
– they often wonder or say, "Who could like me?" or "I don't deserve to be liked";
– they often wonder or say, "Who could love me?" or "I don't deserve to be loved" (referring to "love" in general, not just romantic love).

On the other hand, someone who is more or less immune tends to be generous and open with feelings, and believes "I'm loved (liked) and I deserve to be" ("love" used in its broadest sense, not just referring to romantic love). When you have self-esteem you can also say, "I like (love) myself" and really mean it without feeling stuck-up, self-centered, or silly.

You don't have to love or like yourself all the time. But if you rarely or never do, or if you really don't see how anyone else could feel positive emotions about you, you're at risk. If you can't feel anything for other people, you have a clue that you're building a protective cocoon around yourself. Eating disorders could provide the thread with which you'd weave that cocoon.

At this point you probably have a keener sense than before you began reading this chapter of how the components of your self-image are working to help you be the person you want to be, or are hindering your efforts to grow and mature in a certain direction. The Self-Esteem Test is a final self-check, a quick way to summarize the things discussed up to now, another way to pinpoint areas of possible concern for you.

The Self-Esteem Test

Choose the statement that best describes you.
Most of the time, do you

a. Accept compliments?

b. Negate them?

a. Consider the total picture of who you are and what you've accomplished?

b. Look for the blemishes (errors) in that total picture and dwell on them?

a. Like things about your physical self?

b. Look for and point out your physical shortcomings?

a. Reach a goal and savor it?

b. Reach a goal and think you could have done better or should have done more?

a. Like your friends and seek them out?

b. Tolerate your friends or try to avoid them?

a. Prefer the company of others?

b. Prefer solitude?

If you checked all the *a*'s in the Self-Esteem Test, chances are you have self-esteem and your self-image is probably in fine shape. If you checked all the *b*'s, you need to work on developing self-esteem, and you may be at risk for developing an eating disorder. If you checked some of each, ask yourself why you checked the *b* item rather than the *a* item. You see, sometimes eating disorders can fill in the voids in your life and become a substitute for self-esteem. That's not the direction in which you should be heading if you can help it.

Being comfortable with who you are, liking yourself, having a body-image you can live with even if it's not perfect, being able to take some risks in life and not being overwhelmed at the thought of failure, giving yourself credit when you deserve it — all lead to self-esteem and come from having a realistic self-image and a self-perception based on fact rather than fantasy. They're very important qualities to have, and when they're present there's less room in your psyche for the thought processes that lead to eating disorders.

2
THE TERRIBLE TRANSFORMATION

When Habits Become Obsessions, Compulsions, or Addictions

I know it's weird, but I knock wood every time I talk about something good that's happened. I'm not always aware I'm doing it until a friend says, "Why did you just do that?"

Mary Z., age fifteen

I smoke two packs of cigarettes a day. It started out as something I wanted to do because I thought it made me look older and sexy. Now I don't want to do it anymore and I find I can't not do it.

Tanya P., age eighteen

Habits are the sorts of behaviors that most of us do over and over again, in the same ways, often under similar circumstances. Just about anything a person can think of doing can turn into a habit. Sometimes we don't know where or when the habits started and sometimes we make conscious choices to do things that then become our habits. Sometimes we're very aware of our habits and depend on them to help us get through each day; at other times we hardly notice them.

Why do we develop habits? The truth is that without

habits our lives might become slightly chaotic; habits impose order and structure, and make it easy to do certain tasks. They also have the potential to enhance self-esteem by making a person feel calm, secure, at ease in various situations even if that person isn't *consciously* aware that habits have anything to do with feeling that way.

Although having habits, per se, doesn't lead to having an eating disorder, some habits can contribute to the formation of eating disorders. Under certain circumstances, then, habits can break the bounds of being helpful or comfortable actions and become destructive forces that can be physically and emotionally harmful to us. When that occurs, the habits have a negative ripple effect that extends outward to our network of relationships with family, friends, teachers, employers, and even casual acquaintances. The bottom line is that our habits have the potential to be very powerful forces for good or bad in our lives.

How Behaviors Become Habits

Take a moment to think about how you live your life each day. You'll soon realize that it's loaded with habits, from the way you roll out of bed and how you squeeze the toothpaste from the tube to the way you fluff your pillow and arrange your covers before going to sleep at night. Little habits that seem inconsequential separately actually are quite important as a group: they're part of what makes you unique and they're also part of what makes you a civilized, social human being. Habits develop from once-in-a-while behaviors that have become useful to you for some reason. If they weren't useful they wouldn't have become habits — you wouldn't repeat the action enough times to make it a consistent part of your life! So, just about anything you might do has the potential to become a habit if the conditions are right.

What are those conditions? It depends. Habits develop

in a context. That means someone or something triggers them: a feeling, a situation, a time of day, a person, a place. You react to whatever the trigger is with a behavior of some sort.

- A baby is hungry or scared or lonely. The baby reacts to those feelings of stress by sucking its thumb. That thumb-sucking behavior becomes a habit and can persist long after the stress has passed, long after the child grows old enough to discuss things and seek other solutions.

- A teenager hangs out with a certain group of friends in high school and they give each other a "high sign" with their hands every time they pass each other in the halls. As an adult, this person gives the same "high sign" to his colleagues at work — it has become his habit, a signal for him that stands for good feelings, good relationships.

- You get praise as a child for eating everything that you're served at mealtimes. You develop the habit of cleaning your plate even if you're not hungry, because the memory of the praise feels better than the discomfort of an overfull stomach. You then teach this same behavior to your children.

Habits, then, develop in response to something, but they also result in something. What that result is — the impact — is also highly variable.

The Impact of Habits

The impact of habits varies from totally positive to completely negative. They may take the edge off a tense situation, make you feel part of a crowd, get you noticed, help you get a job done efficiently. Habits can enhance your physical and emotional well-being. On the other hand, they can be enormously destructive in the long run, especially if they're the kinds of behaviors that you can lose control of.

One way to analyze a habit's impact is to visualize a

continuum, a line that represents the range of possible ways any behavior (or series of behaviors) can have an impact on your life.

The Habit-Impact Continuum

has positive impact	rarely interferes, minor annoyance	sometimes interferes or annoys	often interferes or annoys	has harmful, destructive impact

The extremes (endpoints) of the continuum are opposites, "positive impact" and "harmful, destructive impact." In between the two extremes there is always a broad and variable range of possible ways habits can affect you. The diagram shows a few of these ways.

Many habits have a positive impact, or are virtually harmless with just a minor annoyance rating. When was the last time that twirling your hair between your fingers or wearing your lucky outfit when you took an exam interfered with anything else you did? It's not likely such habits ever would. It's more likely that they'd be useful to you in some way: for example, as tension relievers. Some habits, especially those that are common courtesies — holding the door open for the person behind you, waiting for everyone at the table to be served before starting to eat, saying "thank you" when someone does something for you — usually result in similar courtesies and other nice things coming your way.

Some habits are harmless at certain times and harmful at other times.

In junior high school we were allowed to chew gum in class, so I chewed gum today when I got to homeroom. How was

I to know this high school doesn't let you? My teacher came
down all over me, made me march up to the front of the
room and deposit the gum in the waste can. She made a
real fool of me.

Andrea C., age fifteen

I jiggle my foot and leg a lot when I have to sit still at a
desk. Today my foot slipped, I fell over backwards in the
chair, knocked into the kid behind me, and got sent to the
dean of students for disrupting the class. They thought I did
it on purpose.

Todd R., age thirteen

Unfortunately, some habits start out as once-in-a-while
behaviors and turn into activities that dominate your thoughts
to such an extreme that you become obsessed with them, and
once obsessed you feel a compulsion or urge to do them in
spite of knowing better. This is basically what happens with
the dieting patterns of anorectics or the bingeing and purging
behaviors of bulimics.

Since starting college last fall I've become a junk-food ad-
dict. Lately, all I can think about when I'm supposed to be
studying is eating; I get crabby and frustrated when I can't
get a quick food fix. I'm spending a load of money I can't
afford to keep myself in food, and my grades are starting to
slip. I recently learned how to vomit the stuff I eat, because
otherwise I feel really sick. I've been afraid to talk to anyone about this because I think they'll laugh. Everyone junks
out. So why should it be such a problem for me?

Corinne M., age eighteen

You may become physically addicted if the habit is something
like drinking alcohol, smoking, or recreational drug use-
turned-abuse.

CATHY
COPYRIGHT 1986 UNIVERSAL PRESS SYNDICATE.
Reprinted with permission. All rights reserved.

In general, if

- a habit becomes so important in your life that you can't or won't function without using it as a crutch,
- you can't go for a reasonable amount of time without feeling an intense, inner pressure to perform that behavior,
- it peppers your thoughts to an unnatural degree,

then the habit has flipped into the harmful range and it's no longer technically just a habit. It's something much stronger and much more central to your existence, which could be an *obsession* (an idea or thought that persists even though you may not want it to), a *compulsion* (something you need to do over and over without really understanding why), or an *addiction* (a craving due to a physical and emotional dependency on substances like alcohol, nicotine, or drugs). Such behaviors are like habits gone crazy, out of control and very hard to stop. They can throw your normal life-style off balance, damage your physical and mental health, and make life miserable for the friends and relatives around you.

Once the habit is transformed into something that controls you rather than something you can control, the impact is clearly destructive. At that stage, it can be very hard for a person to regain control without professional counseling or medical intervention.

Your Personal Habit Profile

Since habits are such personal, individualized behaviors, it's important to remember that how good or bad, safe or unsafe, useful or destructive a habit is depends in large part on the person who has the habit and the context of the habit. What's right for another person might not be right for you. What someone else can easily handle and control might turn into an obsession or compulsion for you. Or vice versa. No two people's personal habit profiles will look exactly alike. As you grow and mature, your reactions to things like school or work, social life, family, and so on, change so it's not unusual for any one person's habit profile to look different from one period of time to another.

A personal habit profile is a chart of your habits and the impact they have on your life. Most of us have several habits, some of which we'd rather not have but which don't interfere with anything else so we don't make an effort to change them, some of which we'd like to change but can't or won't, and some of which we choose consciously to maintain. The ideal situation is to be aware of your habits and keep them in balance so that they won't fall toward the unsafe part of that habit-impact continuum.

Creating your personal habit profile can actually

- help you focus on your everyday behaviors and recognize things about yourself that might have slipped your notice;
- help you focus on how you think and talk about yourself;
- help you see whether or not your habits are placing you on a self-destructive path;
- give you insight into what's going on in your life right now and why.

To develop this personal habit profile, you first sort out the habits you have. Once that's done, you can place them on a habit-impact continuum and you'll have created your personal habit profile.

How can you uncover your habits? Try the Habit Hunter Exercise and the Daily Activities Awareness Exercise to help you find them.

The Habit Hunter Exercise

Imagine that you're a scientist about to study a one-of-a-kind animal: yourself. Since no other creature on earth has ever been exactly like you, your task is to devise an accurate accounting of the things you do that make you unique and probably help your species survive. To make your job easier, you've been given a videotape of yourself which was made without your knowledge. It has several scenes:

1. You're getting ready for school/work in the morning.
2. You're on your way to school/work.
3. You're in your favorite class at school./You're doing your favorite task at work.
4. You're in your worst class at school./You're doing your least favorite task at work.
5. You're having a meal.
6. You're doing what you like to do after school/work.
7. You're doing homework./You've had to take work home from your job.
8. You're relaxing at home in the evening.
9. You're talking with family members.
10. You're talking with friends.

What do you see happening during each scene on the tape?

As you imagine yourself watching this tape with a scientist's sharp eye for detail, actually write down all the habits you think you'd see happening per scene. Indicate any positive or negative effects of the habits on you and anyone you're with, if and how people reacted to your habits, and what you think triggered each habit.

The Daily Activities Awareness Exercise

Actually spend a day observing yourself. Start from the moment you get up on an average (i.e., a school or work) day.

Have a small note pad (like an assignment book) and pen by your clock so you can start recording your habits from the moment you get up. Take the pad with you to school or work, and jot down the habits that occur when you're there. Ask your friends and teachers (employer) whether they've noticed any of your habits and, if so, what they are.

Compare your results from these two exercises. Are the habits you imagined happening the same types of behaviors that really did occur during your day of self-observation? Using the information you've just developed about your habits, fill in the following personal habit continuum to come up with your personal habit profile:

Personal Habit Profile

has positive impact	rarely interferes, minor annoyance	sometimes interferes or annoys	often interferes or annoys	has harmful, destructive impact

Decoding Your Results

If you're satisfied with your personal habit profile, congratulations. But what happens if your habit profile isn't a good one, if the majority of things appear in the less-desirable categories? Does that mean your habits are out of control? Does it mean you're on the road to developing an obsession, compulsion, or addiction? Should you worry?

The answers to these questions are, in each case, "It depends." Here's why: habits must be evaluated in the context of where and when they occur and what triggers them, and a habit profile is changeable. With that in mind ask yourself, "How long have I had these problematic habits?" (if you can't remember a time when they weren't part of your life, you may have a real problem) and "Can I continue to live like this or are the habits making my life and everyone else's really uncomfortable?" (if you're uncomfortable, there's a problem that needs correcting).

The Bottom Line Question

The bottom line question is "Who's in control? You or the habit?" When habits move in the direction of obsessions, compulsions, or addictions, it may feel like they have lives of their own. Their impact is negative. When any habit or group of habits is in control of you, you may look at life differently from the way you have in the past. You may find yourself paying more attention to the thing you're obsessed with than you do to your friends, family, and school or work-related responsibilities. You may find that your interests begin to become narrowly focused and eventually end up focused *only* on whatever it is that obsesses you. Your activities will become geared to satisfying that obsession, so what you actually do will appear compulsive, illogical, and bizarre and will be very resistant to change — either at someone else's suggestion or by your own attempts.

People who *don't* have obsessions, compulsions, or addictions tend to have communication styles and habits that make it more comfortable and easier to relate to other people who make up their network of friends, family, and acquaintances. A diagram of how they operate looks like a system of interlocking circles:

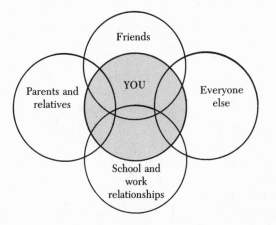

There's overlap between the circles, which means in real life there's give-and-take among the different people in the network.

But the diagram looks different if your habits turn into obsessions, compulsions, or addictions. Instead of all overlapping circles, the one that represents "you" moves to a different position, as though you were in an outside orbit.

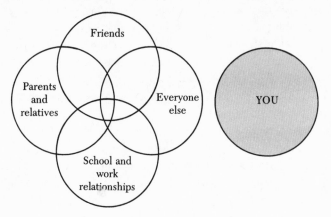

The person and the obsession, compulsion, or addiction become as one — isolated, alone, and cut off from everything or everyone else that used to be a meaningful part of life.

Habits Transformed into Eating Disorders

As we've seen, habits do not necessarily *lead* to obsessive behavior — we all have habits. But understanding habits can help us see when we are becoming obsessed. Obsessive behaviors or habits are signs that something is wrong. And when an obsession or compulsion has to do with food and eating, then an eating disorder is developing.

When someone develops an eating disorder, a number of habits flip from the normal range to the destructive end of the continuum. Eating habits change drastically. In anorexia, food is not seen as life-sustaining, but an enemy to be avoided at all costs. At the same time, the anorectic becomes obsessed with the food that can't be consumed. With bulimia, cravings for certain foods develop into behaviors that mimic physical addictions. So, with anorexia and bulimia, normal eating habits are replaced by obsessive thoughts about food and the compulsive dieting or bingeing and purging — acts that temporarily ease and satisfy the obsessions.

Relationships suffer. Communication with friends, family, and other people stops being two-way and sometimes stops altogether. Isolation is preferred to socialization, and the barriers to interacting with the people who make up your network of relationships are created.

Melinda P., a sixteen-year-old who had been anorectic and bulimic for two years before receiving professional therapy, discussed how the eating disorder affected her and called the description a "blanketing fog scenario." Here's part of it:

The more I got into the dieting, and later on the more I binged and threw up, the less I cared about other things or people. Nothing mattered except that diet or the binge. I actually forgot how to have fun with friends. I never talked much to my parents anyway, but when I was really into the anorexia and bulimia stuff I cut them out of my life completely. I even built a barrier between the door of my room and my bed — where I spend most of my time — with my desk, on top of which I piled dozens of books about cooking, nutrition, even how to grow fruits and vegetables. It was my private fortress. The longer I did my thing, the more I felt like I was moving around in a fog — a blanketing fog that could shield me from everyone and everything I used to want to be around. That fog feeling was really weird. I honestly believed no one would notice my habits had changed, because I thought no one would see through that fog. That lasted for months. But everyone noticed, and you know what's funny, no one *could* crack through that fog for a long time. It was like being in a womb. Or a tomb.

The transformation of habits into obsessions, compulsions, or addictions is often terrible, but it doesn't have to be terminal. In the chapters that follow, we'll see how and why this is true for eating disorders.

3
STRAIGHT FACTS ABOUT ANOREXIA NERVOSA

When Not Eating Becomes Your Obsession

In many ways anorexia is stronger than grief, more abiding than love.

— Sandra H. Heater,
Am I Still Visible?

What Is Anorexia Nervosa?

Anorexia nervosa is a dangerous eating disorder that can harm its victims physically and mentally as they starve themselves in a quest for thinness. *Anorexia* means "loss of appetite," but that's misleading — its victims are almost always hungry and through sheer willpower deny that hunger and learn to suppress it, sometimes even reveling in it as proof of their strength and self-control.

Who Gets It?

Anorexia nervosa affects many more females than males, and many more teens than adults. Some estimates suggest there are about 150,000 American females between the ages of twelve and twenty-five who are anorectic; others suggest that between 1 and 4 percent of high school girls are. Of the people who are anorectic, only about one in fifteen is male. The fact is that there are no exact figures, and no matter what the numbers are, a large proportion of young people have suffered from the negative effects of anorexia nervosa. Those people include singer Pat Boone's daughter Cherry Boone O'Neill, actresses Ally Sheedy and Sandra Dee, and singer Karen Carpenter (who died as a result of complications caused by both anorexia and bulimia).

What Causes It?

There's never just one cause of anorexia. It can be triggered by a combination of factors — family problems, romantic relationship problems, someone else's casual remarks about your physical shape. It can be a reaction to growing up in an environment where you had to eat everything you were served and weren't allowed to express your preferences. It can develop from a lifelong habit of dieting and a belief system that equates thinness with success and happiness. It may be the ticket you're looking for that you think will make you part of the "in crowd" at your school. It may be your way of getting back at a parent, proving something, getting yourself noticed. You may be very aware of the possible causes or completely oblivious to them, and you may begin your quest for thinness voluntarily and completely aware of what you're doing, or you might find yourself trapped in the eating-disorder maze without understanding how it happened. Whether it happens by choice or by chance is a question that isn't always answerable, but it's often a combination of both choice and chance. To the extent that there *are* elements of choice involved, you can do something to prevent or address the problem.

How Can Eating Disorders Be Prevented?

The easiest way to prevent something from becoming an issue in your life is to deal with it *before* it has a chance to become a problem. This is called primary prevention. You accomplish it by educating yourself about a topic so that you have accurate facts at your disposal, can figure out the probable risks that might pop up in a situation you could find yourself in, and are prepared to act accordingly. Examples of this kind of prevention are wearing a seat belt when you drive or ride in a car, using suntan lotion with a high sunscreen factor to keep from getting burned your first day at the beach, or not doing drugs because you know they can be physically harmful or even addictive.

Primary prevention of eating disorders (both anorexia and bulimia) can be accomplished by trying any or all of the following suggestions.

1. Read current books and articles about eating disorders.

That way, you'll learn about warning signs and symptoms, find out what anorexia nervosa and bulimia can do to you, and make informed choices about ways to avoid the problem.

2. Don't hang out with a crowd of people who are into the habits of excessive dieting or bingeing and purging.

If you don't run in those circles, you'll be less likely to think what they do is the norm and you might not be pressured or tempted to try what they're doing.

3. Don't get a job in a food-related business if you think you might be susceptible to developing an eating disorder.

Waiting tables, short-order cooking, catering, delivering pizzas, and dishing out ice cream at an ice cream parlor are the kinds of jobs that may foster an obsession and turn it into a full-blown eating disorder.

4. Don't judge yourself against the standard of beauty put forth in fashion magazines, in the movies, or on TV.

Very few people are as perfect as they look in print or on film.

5. Don't keep a scale in your room or bathroom or anywhere you can get to it easily.

If you know, for example, that seeing a fluctuation in your weight is a downer for you, simply don't weigh yourself!

6. Don't eat a lot of junk foods.

Recent research suggests there might be a chemical basis for eating disorders — in certain people, high-calorie, high-carbohydrate foods can trigger the bulimic cycle.

7. Only buy clothes that fit well (within the limits of the style you're aiming for).

For instance, clothes that are so tight you can't sit or breathe comfortably in them are bound to make you feel "fat" even if you're not. Similarly, don't buy things that you plan to "get into" in a matter of weeks or months, because you might not *ever* achieve that size. On the other hand, if you wear clothes that make you feel good, you get an external confidence boost that can be positively preventive!

8. Put yourself in situations where you can develop your communication skills, have a sense of control, feel good about what you do, and see the positive results of your efforts.

Join a YMCA leadership club and train to be a volunteer. Babysit after school for working parents who really need your help. Be a coach for younger kids. Help an elderly neighbor on a steady basis. When other people appreciate you, your self-confidence soars, you can begin to appreciate yourself, and there's little reason to use an eating disorder as a way of saying, "Notice me" or as a way of trying to assert control over people.

9. Eat when you're hungry; don't force yourself to eat when you're not, and don't let anyone else force you, either.

As long as you can accurately read the hunger-fullness signals your body sends out and respond to them appropriately, you're less likely to fall victim to an eating disorder than if you consistently ignore what your body is telling you.

10. If something's on your mind, speak up.

Being up-front about yourself, speaking out, and making your position clear when there's something (good or bad) you feel should be aired will prevent your need to use an eating disorder as an emotional shield, as a way to avoid communication, or as a substitute for it.

All of these pointers can be summarized in one simple equation: PREVENTION = EDUCATION + MOTIVATION + CONTROL. Remember, this applies to preventing any eating disorder.

How Do You Know Whether You Have Anorexia?

The Eating Attitudes Test, which follows, developed by Drs. David Garner and Paul Garfinkel, has been used since 1979 as a quick and reliable way to determine if you have the symptoms of anorexia nervosa. Take the test. All you have to do is indicate (for each statement) which of the following terms best describes you: "Always," "Very Often," "Often," "Sometimes," "Rarely," or "Never."

1. Like eating with other people.
2. Prepare foods for others but don't eat what I cook.
3. Become anxious prior to cooking.
4. Am terrified about being overweight.
5. Avoid eating when I am hungry.
6. Find myself preoccupied with food.
7. Have gone on eating binges where I feel that I may not be able to stop.
8. Cut my food into small pieces.
9. Aware of the calorie content of foods that I eat.
10. Particularly avoid foods with a high carbohydrate content (such as bread, potatoes, rice, etc.).
11. Feel bloated after meals.
12. Feel that others would prefer if I ate more.
13. Vomit after I have eaten.
14. Feel extremely guilty after eating.
15. Am preoccupied with a desire to be thinner.
16. Exercise strenuously to burn off calories.
17. Weigh myself several times a day.
18. Like my clothes to fit tightly.
19. Enjoy eating meat.

20. Wake up early in the morning.
21. Eat the same foods day after day.
22. Think about burning up calories when I exercise.
23. Have regular menstrual periods.
24. Other people think that I am too thin.
25. Am preoccupied with the thought of having fat on my body.
26. Take longer than others to eat my meals.
27. Enjoy eating at restaurants.
28. Take laxatives.
29. Avoid foods with sugar in them.
30. Eat diet foods.
31. Feel that food controls my life.
32. Display self-control around food.
33. Feel that others pressure me to eat.
34. Give too much time and thought to food.
35. Suffer from constipation.
36. Feel uncomfortable eating sweets.
37. Engage in dieting behavior.
38. Like my stomach to be empty.
39. Enjoy trying new foods.
40. Have the impulse to vomit after meals.

(Source: D. M. Garner and P. E. Garfinkel, "The Eating Attitudes Test: An Index of the Symptoms of Anorexia Nervosa," *Psychological Medicine,* 9[1979]: 278.)

If you replied, "Never" to questions 1, 18, 19, 23 (if you are a girl), and 39 and "Always" to all the others, yours are the most *symptomatic* responses and strongly suggest you have a full-blown problem with anorexia. Whatever your answers are, you can use them as an index to determine if you have a problem and how deep it is, and as a way to pinpoint the areas that are most troublesome and that you might need to get some professional help in dealing with.

What Does Anorexia Do to You?

Anorexia makes you obsessive about *not* gaining weight. Weighing yourself several times a day is an occasion for joy (if weight has been lost) or despair (if the scale shows a gain). Because of this you're likely to look at yourself constantly in mirrors to check the contours of your body, paying particular attention to the size of your hips, thighs, and stomach (and breasts if you're a girl). If you've lost a very large proportion of your total body weight — 20 to 25 percent — you may actually see an obese, bloated person in the mirror, because such extreme weight loss causes chemical changes in your brain, which alter your perception and make you see fat where there is none. To hide the imagined fat you'll probably start wearing hugely oversized clothes, not just fashionably large things.

You hate fat (maybe even fear it), so you deny yourself the right to eat the way most people do. You may ban red meats and processed meats (such as bologna and hot dogs) from your diet altogether, restrict yourself to eating small amounts of white meat, poultry, and nonfatty fish. You cut out foods such as mayonnaise, peanut butter, hard cheeses, butter, and margarine, and avoid sweets and desserts, processed breads and sugary cereals. If confronted, you justify your choices by saying you know a lot about nutrition and you're just "eating healthy" by cutting down fats and cholesterol in your diet. You probably allow yourself certain "safe" foods such as low-calorie vegetables, crunchy fruits such as apples, salads with vinegar or no-oil diet salad dressings, plain popcorn, unsalted rice cakes, low-fat cottage cheese, and non-fat yogurt, but only in limited amounts. This doesn't mean you're not interested in food, though. Quite the contrary — you're likely to get really involved with every aspect of food: purchase, preparation, and feeding, but for others, not for yourself.

> When I was at my very worst — I think I got down to 82 pounds and I'm 5'7" — I bought my mom two James Beard cookbooks, one Julia Child, and an encyclopedia of Japanese cooking. I also charged a $250 meat order on my mom's credit card from a mail-order beef company's Christmas catalogue. For two months I prepared every single dinner at home and made all the brown-bag lunches for my little brother and sister. I wouldn't let them near the refrigerator. I felt like the kitchen was all mine. I ate no more than 250 calories a day and kept a notebook about what I ate. I must have really wanted to torture myself. When we were in family therapy one evening, my mom said I was like a drug pusher only I was a food pusher.
>
> *Antoinette L., age seventeen*

Sometimes you lose your self-control and start to binge, flipping yourself into a bulimic pattern that makes you feel guilty and scared. So you purge, the way a bulimic would, and then go back to your anorectic habits. This is so common that researchers David C. Sibley and Barton J. Blinder report that 45 to 50 percent of patients with anorexia nervosa engage in binge eating and vomiting (Source: "Anorexia Nervosa," in *The Eating Disorders*, p. 254. New York: PMA Publishing, 1988). This seesaw routine can go on indefinitely, but sometimes it just goes away. There are some fortunate people whose eating disorders disappear after being a real problem, even if they haven't received any therapy.

As you get more and more obsessed with losing weight,

CATHY
COPYRIGHT 1986 UNIVERSAL PRESS SYNDICATE.
Reprinted with permission. All rights reserved.

and as you get more and more frightened of eating, your personality changes:

> My brother saw the movie *Ghostbusters* and told me that I was like Sigourney Weaver in the film. He said I'd been invaded by a powerful demon like she was supposed to have been, and that mine was the anorexia. He said he wished there were anorexia busters. He was only nine at the time. You know, he was right.
>
> *Larrayne O., age sixteen*

You'll probably develop rituals to enable you to do even the most ordinary things and to divert your attention from your physical hunger and discomfort. You may need to touch a certain piece of furniture before walking out the door, make yourself do one hundred sit-ups for each bite of food you allow yourself to eat, only be able to swallow food after you've chewed each mouthful a set number of times, not allow an eating utensil to touch your lips, and so on. You tend to get very strict with yourself and everyone else about these things and don't like anyone to interfere with you when you're performing your rituals. You also lose your sense of humor as you become a rigid person doing the same things in the same ways, unvaryingly. In some people this rigidity shows up in handwriting that becomes uncharacteristically small and neat, or is reflected in drawings that become extremely detailed.

Maintaining rituals, keeping your mind off your hunger, and sticking to the commitment to lose weight when you don't need to take a lot of time and energy. You lose tolerance for things and people you used to like. You become very self-centered and choose to isolate yourself as much as possible. When you do reach out and try to spend time with other people you can alienate them easily — if you ask for advice you're likely to reject it immediately; your opinions have to be accepted or you get insulted; you can't quite see someone else's point of view and may not even want to. You may stop taking your phone calls, refuse to go out with friends, and eventually you may refuse to go out at all — skipping school, not going to work. Your whole routine changes as your personality and sense of identity become enmeshed with the anorexia and all your efforts are geared to maintaining the eating disorder. Sleeping often becomes a problem, in part because it can be painful to lie down — if you've lost too much weight, there's not enough fat left on your body to cushion your bones. You may be cold all the time and may find that moving around a lot helps, so you become compulsive about exercising.

As you lose more and more weight (especially if you reach that dangerous mark of 20 to 25 percent of your acceptable, "normal" weight) your body undergoes some dramatic physical changes. Your face and body take on a "concentration camp" appearance. Your eyes may seem vacant and hollow, your bones protrude, and your stomach and chest seem to cave in. Your hair falls out and you may develop fine, downy hair (lanugo) on other parts of your body. Your skin changes in color and texture — it gets dry and rough, sometimes purplish or darker than normal in color, and your fingernails take on a bluish tinge. This same tinge may extend from above your wristbones to your fingertips and from above your kneecaps to your toes. Sometimes your fingernails develop ridges. If you don't have enough fat on your body, your muscles are used up for food and fuel, so your muscle tone decreases. You may experience pain in your muscles, joints, and bones; such pain can mean that you have developed osteoporosis ("brittle bones") as a result of the self-starvation and actually have stress fractures in those bones. If you're female, your periods may stop (or not start at all if you hadn't menstruated before you developed anorexia nervosa). You may have constipation problems. Many anorectics report losing their sexual feelings and sex drives.

Anorexia changes you physically, alters your personality, and also changes the way other people relate and react to you. When you're severely emaciated, people who haven't seen you for a while may actually pull away from you when you meet, afraid of what they're observing, unsure of how to react. People who are in touch with you on a regular basis often vacillate between being overly kind and sweet, treating you as if you were very feeble and fragile, and trying a "get tough" tactic with you, trying to convince you to give up your anorexia, threatening, ranting, and fighting with you.

Things can go from bad to worse at home, especially if you have brothers or sisters. They may be jealous of the attention you're getting because you're anorectic. They may try to drive a wedge between you and your parents in order to get some of that attention for themselves. If they're little, they may try to mimic what you do at mealtimes. If they're older, they may taunt you. Instead of having siblings to support you, you may end up with siblings who try to sabotage you. Your parents can even get into battles with each other about you. They may not agree on how to handle you. One parent may feel left out if you seem to be closer to the other. Their own relationship may suffer because of the anorexia and they may try to make you feel guilty and responsible for their problems.

With anorexia, you lose the ability to see yourself as others see you:

> When I saw home movies of myself during the worst of my anorexia period I couldn't believe it. It felt like I was looking at some horror film, something that could have been titled *The Last of the Zombies* or *The Walking, Talking, Waking Dead*. I really had no idea that I was so far gone. I must have been in one heck of a self-perception pickle (see, I'm still thinking about food!).
>
> *Emilee Z., age sixteen*

You may have trouble understanding or agreeing with others' concerns for your health and well-being. You think you're on your way to achieving a very important goal and assume everyone who challenges you is jealous. You're able to ignore the reactions and rejection of people who have been part of your life, because the anorexia makes you believe you're strong and superior, in spite of the fact that others see and say that it's making you ill. However physically ill or weak you feel when you're starving yourself this way, however lonely and isolated you are, such things are secondary to the sense of power you believe you have over yourself and your hunger, and because they're secondary you don't try to fix them:

> You know how everyone's talking about designer drugs these days? I'm not into drugs, but I have anorexia to help me get through each day. That's my designer eating disorder. It's for the elite. Not everyone can stick with it and prove what they're made of. I can.
>
> *Meredith McG., age eighteen,*
> *at her first therapy session*
> *for treatment of anorexia nervosa*

strength!

That sense of control and power will feed you (in the absence of actual food), will give you the impetus to continue in your disordered patterns.

Ironically, though, if you're anorectic, it's the anorexia that has the real control over you. You're trapped. The anorexia makes you think everyone else is the enemy and anorexia is your ally — a perspective that's very tough to challenge and change. That's why fighting anorexia nervosa can be so hard — it feels like you're fighting yourself. The emotional anguish and conflict many anorectics struggle with as they decide what to do is poignantly reflected in a letter sent to me anonymously by one reader of *When Food's a Foe*:

> You are *so* right — anorexics have bad self-images and that's how they start and continue. I admit I have a terrible self-image. My self keeps saying, "CAN'T YOU DO ANYTHING RIGHT?" in a loud voice, every time I do the *slightest* thing wrong, like dial the wrong number, hit all the red lights, forget the slightest detail, or forget a word I'd like to use.
>
> You are *so* right — yes, I've lost the control in my life, I need to be thinner to get it back. . . . I need control, I've become very precise — you can tell my writing has become a little neater. . . . Sorry, I really am, but I need to do this.

I feel terrible and rejected and I want to cry — Food is my
out because Food is my Foe.

Is It Worth Fighting?

The answer is yes. You may not believe this or agree with it
now, but having anorexia nervosa is not a desirable state to
be in. It can kill you. So, truthfully, the risks outweigh whatever benefits you think there are in being anorectic. It takes
strength and tenacity to be anorectic, and that same strength
and tenacity can be used to free yourself of anorexia. It's not
always easy, as another reader of *When Food's a Foe* wrote
to me as she began to recover from anorexia:

> Every day the food obsession is becoming less and less im-
> portant to me. I have to admit that some days are pretty
> bad, but those days are occurring less frequently. I'm really
> happy with my progress and I WILL NOT start going back-
> wards. I'm too important to be on the verge of death.

Fighting anorexia isn't easy, but it's definitely worth it, and
one of the payoffs is when you can say and believe, "I'm too
important to be doing this to myself."

4
STRAIGHT FACTS
ABOUT BULIMIA

When Bingeing and Purging
Becomes Your Obsession

What Is Bulimia?

Bulimia is another eating disorder that can be harmful to your physical and mental health. Like anorexia, it is fueled and propelled by a dual obsession — thinness and food. In fact, these two eating disorders have been called "Cinderella's stepsisters" and are often referred to as flip sides of the same coin. Unlike anorexia, though, which prompts you to starve yourself, bulimia (which means "ox hunger") is most often a binge-purge pattern, in which you feel an overwhelming urge to binge (to eat a large amount of food in a short period of time) and then an equally overwhelming need to purge (to eliminate) from your body whatever foods you've eaten during your binge. The method you choose to purge may be self-induced vomiting, excessive use of laxatives, use of emetics, which make you vomit, use of diuretics (pills that rid your body of water), enemas, diet pills, or any combination of these. Some bulimics actually chew their food and then spit it out without swallowing it in order to avoid gaining weight. Some don't even purge but just alternate between binges and barely eating at all. This form of the eating disorder is called nonpurging bulimia, and what it has in common with bulimia nervosa is that in addition to the binges, you are preoccupied with your body's shape and your weight, you exercise to extreme or diet and/or fast — all to prevent weight gain, and when you're in the midst of a binge, you feel as if you have little or no control over your eating behavior.

Who Gets It?

Bulimia affects many more females than males, and it's more common among older teenagers than younger ones. The average age for bulimia to start is around eighteen, just when you'd go off to college or strike out on your own, perhaps getting a job and your own place to live. Bulimia is rampant on college campuses, where people live in close contact in dorms and can learn about bingeing and vomiting from one another and pick up the habit quite quickly. College athletes are known to be especially at risk. The June 13, 1986, issue of *American Medical News* reported that a study of female athletes at Michigan State University found 74 percent of gymnasts, 45 percent of long-distance runners, 50 percent of field hockey players, and 25 percent of varsity softball, volleyball, and tennis players and track runners used "drastic dieting" methods (the methods bulimics use to purge), believing their athletic performance would improve if they were thin, unaware of the health risks. But males too are at risk, especially if they play sports in which weight classes are important. A recent study investigating weight control in teenagers made an alarming discovery: 45 percent of teenagers who didn't have any other symptoms of eating disorders abused laxatives in order to achieve weight loss, with slightly more guys than girls doing this (Source: J. L. Lachenmeyer et al., "Laxative Abuse for Weight Control in Adolescents," *International Journal of Eating Disorders*, 7, no. 6 [November 1988]: 849–52). This is scary and serious because laxative abuse coupled with dieting and focus on low weight can develop into the kinds of thought and behavior patterns that let bulimia take hold and dominate a person's life for years. Indeed, there are many adult bulimics for whom bulimia is a chronic (long-lasting or recurring) problem.

Recently, it seems, younger teens are getting hooked. A survey of tenth-grade students published in 1986 found that 13 percent of them reported purging behavior (of the girls surveyed, 10.6 percent vomited, 6.8 percent used laxatives, 3.6 percent used diuretics), with females outnumbering male purgers two to one (Source: Joel D. Killen et al., "Self Induced Vomiting and Laxative and Diuretic Use among Teenagers," *JAMA*, 255, no. 11: 1447). Other researchers who've surveyed ninth through twelfth graders have come up with similar results. So the trend seems to be that bulimia is filtering down from the college age groups to high school age groups. The fact is that there are no exact figures, and whatever the numbers, a large proportion of young people have suffered from the negative effects of bulimia. These people include the actress Jane Fonda, Olympic gymnast Cathy Rigby, tennis star Zena Garrison, and, as mentioned, singer Karen Carpenter (who died as a result of complications caused by both anorexia and bulimia).

What Causes It?

There are many possible causes of bulimia. Like anorexia, it can be triggered by family problems, relationship problems, or someone else's casual remarks about your weight and physical appearance. Bulimia often develops after a prolonged period of dieting, and sometimes it follows a period of actually being anorectic. It can be someone's attempt to be part of a group of kids who binge and purge because they believe (mistakenly) that bulimia's the best way to have their cake and eat it too: that is, to eat a lot and not gain weight. In this respect, it can be considered a learned behavior that also happens to be addictive — the more you do it, the more you need to do it and the less control you have to voluntarily stop doing it. If you're an athlete, bulimia may be triggered by the demands of your coach or trainer that you achieve a certain weight goal. It can be a way to cope with a shaky self-image. Stress and tension also seem to be able to provoke bulimia.

In addition, people who suffer from depression (a specific psychological illness marked by symptoms such as losing interest in things they used to love to do, being dejected or feeling hopeless, experiencing changes in how their bodies function, feeling tired out of proportion to their physical activity, having school problems, thinking about suicide) frequently become bulimic, and there seems to be a direct link between the two problems. Genetics may play a role in this depression-bulimia connection; researchers already know that if you've had a close relative who's had depression, this puts you at greater risk of developing the same illness, and they are currently studying the link with bulimia in such cases.

You may find yourself trapped in a bulimic pattern without understanding how you got there or you may be able to point to a specific time, place, or circumstance and be able to say, "That's why I got started; that's how I got hooked on bingeing and purging." It's not always obvious whether bulimia happens by choice or by chance, but it's often a combination of both. To the extent that there *are* elements of choice involved, you can do something to prevent or address the problem.

Primary Prevention

As we discussed in Chapter 3, the easiest way to prevent something from becoming a negative issue in your life is to deal with it *before* it has a chance to become a problem. This is called primary prevention. You might want to refer back to pages 42 through 44 to refresh your memory about things to try that could help you avoid getting into an eating-disordered pattern in the first place.

How Do You Know Whether You Have Bulimia?

There are as many kinds of binges and splurges and pig-outs as there are inventive people, so how you define these acts is a very personal thing.

> A binge is a triple banana split (no nuts, extra cherries, whipped cream, and extra fudge sauce in addition to the usual stuff on it). It's how I reward myself when I ace an exam.
>
> *Fred M., age fourteen*

> If I'm going to splurge, I do it by eating those oversized chocolate chip cookies you can get at places like Mrs. Field's or David's Cookies — three or four make up the perfect splurge for me. I do it when I need a little extra boost and have the money to do it for myself!
>
> *Barb V., age fifteen*

> A pig-out is eating anything I want without worrying about the cost or whether it'll make me gain weight or break out. I don't even care what my friends call me! A pig-out in my mind is the freedom to really enjoy what I eat.
>
> *Sarah P., age seventeen*

For these people and others like them, a binge or a splurge or a pig-out is something fun, something to reward themselves with, something that's a pleasurable, guilt-free treat. A binge can be their way of relieving tension or hurt feelings. As long as

CATHY
COPYRIGHT 1986 UNIVERSAL PRESS SYNDICATE.
Reprinted with permission. All rights reserved.

- they're able to say to themselves, "I know why I'm doing this,"
- they don't follow the binge, splurge, or pig-out by purging,
- their binges, splurges, and pig-outs don't interfere with how they live their lives,

such binges are NOT classified as bulimic behavior.

But for other people, a binge is a necessary evil that is experienced almost as a curse or a burden:

> A binge is something I do because I have to, not because I want to. A binge is like some medieval torturer subjecting me to things I wouldn't allow done to myself if I could help it.
>
> *Arlie M., age eighteen*

> A binge? A binge is eating and not tasting. I feel like a trash compactor — shovel it in, smash it, throw it out. Over and over, the same thing. I waste a lot of time and energy on this and I wish I didn't have to.
>
> *Lydia Z., age seventeen*

Bulimic binges aren't pleasurable. They're habit-forming and become dominant forces in your life. They feel terrible — they hurt physically and trigger the need to purge, and all aspects of the binge-purge cycle can make you feel guilty, depressed, and out of control. You may find yourself feeling angry and spacy ("zoned out" is how one person described it), nervous, disgusted with yourself, panicky, lonely, or even inadequate before, during, and after a binge and/or purge episode. Bulimia is probably your problem if a majority of the following statements is true for you:

- "I want to be thin."
- "I have been on diets in the past."
- "I binged without purging for a while before I started bingeing and purging together."
- "I like to eat and I believe I can control my weight by purging."

- "I spend a lot of money each week on foods that most people consider junk."
- "I binge on large amounts of food, which I eat rapidly and may not even really taste."
- "I binge in private."
- "I get anxious about not having enough food around to binge on, so I hoard some in my room."
- "I rarely eat 'three square meals' a day."
- "I prefer to binge in the late afternoons or evenings."
- "I am uncomfortable at the thought of dining in public."
- "I eat even if I'm not hungry."
- "I don't always know when I'm hungry."
- "I have used some or all of the following to control my weight: laxatives, diet pills, water pills, enemas, fasting, vomiting, emetics."
- "I can make myself vomit."
- "I binge and purge at least once a week."
- "I don't feel good about myself for a long time after I binge and purge."
- "I am very impulsive more often than not."
- "I often feel sad or down."
- "I would consider stealing money if I didn't have enough to buy the food for binges."
- "I have a lot of tension in my life that I deal with by bingeing and purging."
- "I know a lot of people who binge and purge."

If you replied "True" to 14 or more of these statements, you probably have a full-blown problem with bulimia. If you answered "True" to 10–13 of these statements, you may be in a pre-bulimic stage — that is, on the verge of developing bulimia. Whatever your answers are, you can use them as an index to determine if you have a problem and how deep your problem is, and as a way to pinpoint the areas you might need to get some professional help in dealing with.

If you feel you need to do some more self-exploration, take the following self-check Bulimia Test (BULIT) developed by Marcia Smith and Mark Thelen to measure the symptoms of bulimia. Answer each question by circling the appropriate letter.

1. Do you ever eat uncontrollably to the point of stuffing yourself (i.e., going on eating binges)?
   a. Once a month or less (or never)
   b. 2–3 times a month
   c. Once or twice a week
   d. 3–6 times a week
   e. Once a day or more

2. I am satisfied with my eating patterns.
   a. Agree
   b. Neutral
   c. Disagree a little
   d. Disagree strongly

3. Have you ever kept eating until you thought you'd explode?
   a. Practically every time I eat
   b. Very frequently
   c. Often
   d. Sometimes
   e. Seldom or never

4. Would you presently call yourself a "binge eater"?
   a. Yes, absolutely
   b. Yes
   c. Yes, probably
   d. Yes, possibly
   e. No, probably not

5. I prefer to eat:
   a. At home alone
   b. At home with others
   c. In a public restaurant
   d. At a friend's house
   e. Doesn't matter

6. Do you feel you have control over the amount of food you consume?
   a. Most or all of the time
   b. A lot of the time
   c. Occasionally
   d. Rarely
   e. Never

7. I use laxatives or suppositories to help control my weight.
   a. Once a day or more
   b. 3–6 times a week
   c. Once or twice a week
   d. 2–3 times a month
   e. Once a month or less (or never)

8. I eat until I feel too tired to continue.
   a. At least once a day
   b. 3–6 times a week
   c. Once or twice a week
   d. 2–3 times a month
   e. Once a month or less (or never)

9. How often do you prefer eating ice cream, milk shakes, or puddings during a binge?
   a. Always
   b. Frequently
   c. Sometimes
   d. Seldom or never
   e. I don't binge

10. How much are you concerned about your eating binges?
    a. I don't binge
    b. Bothers me a little
    c. Moderate concern
    d. Major concern
    e. Probably the biggest concern in my life

11. Most people I know would be amazed if they knew how much food I can consume at one sitting.
    a. Without a doubt
    b. Very probably
    c. Probably
    d. Possibly
    e. No

12. Do you ever eat to the point of feeling sick?
    a. Very frequently
    b. Frequently
    c. Fairly often
    d. Occasionally
    e. Rarely or never

13. I am afraid to eat anything for fear that I won't be able to stop.
    a. Always
    b. Almost always
    c. Frequently
    d. Sometimes
    e. Seldom or never

14. I don't like myself after I eat too much.
    a. Always
    b. Frequently
    c. Sometimes
    d. Seldom or never
    e. I don't eat too much.

15. How often do you intentionally vomit after eating?
    a. 2 or more times a week
    b. Once a week
    c. 2–3 times a month
    d. Once a month
    e. Less than once a month (or never)

16. Which of the following describes your feelings after binge eating?
    a. I don't binge eat
    b. I feel O.K.
    c. I feel mildly upset with myself
    d. I feel quite upset with myself
    e. I hate myself

17. I eat a lot of food when I'm not even hungry.
    a. Very frequently
    b. Frequently
    c. Occasionally
    d. Sometimes
    e. Seldom or never

18. My eating patterns are different from eating patterns of most people.
    a. Always
    b. Almost always
    c. Frequently
    d. Sometimes
    e. Seldom or never

19. I have tried to lose weight by fasting or going on 'crash' diets.
    a. Not in the past year
    b. Once in the past year
    c. 2–3 times in the past year
    d. 4–5 times in the past year
    e. More than 5 times in the past year

20. I feel sad or blue after eating more than I'd planned to eat.
    a. Always
    b. Almost always
    c. Frequently
    d. Sometimes
    e. Seldom, or I don't binge

21. When engaged in an eating binge, I tend to eat foods that are high in carbohydrates (sweets and starches).
    a. Always
    b. Almost always
    c. Frequently
    d. Sometimes
    e. Seldom, or I don't binge

22. Compared to most people, my ability to control my eating behavior seems to be:
    a. Greater than others' ability
    b. About the same
    c. Less
    d. Much less
    e. I have absolutely no control

23. One of your best friends suddenly suggests that you both eat at a new restaurant buffet that night. Although you'd planned on eating something light at home, you go ahead and eat out, eating quite a lot and feeling uncomfortably full. How would you feel about yourself on the ride home?
    a. Fine, glad I'd tried that new restaurant
    b. A little regretful that I'd eaten so much
    c. Somewhat disappointed in myself
    d. Upset with myself
    e. Totally disgusted with myself

24. I would presently label myself a "compulsive eater" (one who engages in episodes of uncontrollable eating).
    a. Absolutely
    b. Yes
    c. Yes, probably
    d. Yes, possibly
    e. No, probably not
25. What is the most weight you've ever lost in 1 month?
    a. Over 20 pounds
    b. 12–20 pounds
    c. 8–11 pounds
    d. 4–7 pounds
    e. Less than 4 pounds
26. If I eat too much at night I feel depressed the next morning.
    a. Always
    b. Frequently
    c. Sometimes
    d. Seldom or never
    e. I don't eat too much at night
27. Do you believe that it is easier for you to vomit than it is for most people?
    a. Yes, it's no problem at all for me
    b. Yes, it's easier
    c. Yes, it's a little easier
    d. About the same
    e. No, it's less easy
28. I feel that food controls my life.
    a. Always
    b. Almost always
    c. Frequently
    d. Sometimes
    e. Seldom or never

29. I feel depressed immediately after I eat too much.
    a. Always
    b. Frequently
    c. Sometimes
    d. Seldom or never
    e. I don't eat too much

30. How often do you vomit after eating in order to lose weight?
    a. Less than once a month (or never)
    b. Once a month
    c. 2–3 times a month
    d. Once a week
    e. 2 or more times a week

31. When consuming a large quantity of food, at what rate of speed do you usually eat?
    a. More rapidly than most people have ever eaten in their lives
    b. A lot more rapidly than most people
    c. A little more rapidly than most people
    d. About the same rate as most people
    e. More slowly than most people (or not applicable)

32. What is the most weight you've ever gained in one month?
    a. Over 20 pounds
    b. 12–20 pounds
    c. 8–11 pounds
    d. 4–7 pounds
    e. Less than 4 pounds

33. Females only. My last menstrual period was
    a. Within the past month
    b. Within the past 2 months
    c. Within the past 4 months
    d. Within the past 6 months
    e. Not within the past 6 months

34. I use diuretics (water pills) to help control my weight.
    a. Once a day or more
    b. 3–6 times a week
    c. Once or twice a week
    d. 2–3 times a month
    e. Once a month or less (or never)
35. How do you think your appetite compares with that of most people you know?
    a. Many times larger than most
    b. Much larger
    c. A little larger
    d. About the same
    e. Smaller than most
36. Females only. My menstrual cycles occur once a month:
    a. Always
    b. Usually
    c. Sometimes
    d. Seldom
    e. Never

How to score your answers:
On #s *1, 2, 6, 10, 16, 19, 22, 23, 30*: 5 points for response *e*, 4 points for *d*'s, 3 points for *c*'s, 2 points for *b*'s, 1 point for *a*'s.
On #s *3–5, 8, 9, 11–15, 17, 18, 20, 21, 24–29, 31, 32, 35*: 5 points for response *a*, 4 points for *b*'s, 3 points for *c*'s, 2 points for *d*'s, 1 point for *e*'s.
Add the scores for all questions except #s 7, 33, 34, and 36. Scores range from 32 to 160; higher scores reflect more serious bulimic symptoms.
(Source: M. C. Smith and M. H. Thelen, "Development and Validation of a Test for Bulimia," *Journal of Consulting and Clinical Psychology*, 52 [1984]: 863–72.)

What Does Bulimia Do to You?

Bulimia makes you obsessive about not gaining weight, but at the same time it makes you obsessive about food — a real dilemma. It makes it just about impossible for you to eat normally. The act of eating isn't something that gives you pleasure, it's not a way to socialize with other people, it's not even a way to keep yourself well nourished and healthy. Bulimia transforms the meaning of food and eating and makes them self-destructive.

You have two warring impulses: you want to be thin and yet you want to eat, but eating can make you gain weight and even become fat. Let's say you're the kind of person who takes the "thin is in/trim is in" cultural bias very seriously. Your eating habits are a little extreme (like those of most teenagers) — you like to binge and then you try to diet after your binges because you do put on some pounds when you binge. Maybe you fast for a day or two or try some over-the-counter diet pills that are sold in groceries and drugstores. But one problem is that when you diet or fast for any extended period of time your metabolism slows down; if you go off the diet and go back to your old eating habits without making any adjustments (like increasing your exercise level moderately) then you're apt to gain weight *faster* because your metabolism is used to burning calories more slowly. So you try dieting again and the same thing happens when you stop. Now you may be more than just a little overweight.

You find out about purging and you decide to try it. You weigh yourself before a big meal and after you've purged, and discover that yes, you've lost a few pounds. The good feeling you get from noting the weight loss is enough to offset any initial distaste you have for vomiting or discomfort you feel from the diarrhea caused by taking too many laxatives or by using an enema. You do this on several occasions, and the more you binge and purge, the easier it becomes for you.

Your early feelings of revulsion or even fear are quickly replaced by the compulsion to repeat these bulimic patterns. You're hooked pretty quickly, and after a while you stop trying to think logically about what you're doing. You just feel like you have to do it.

When that point is reached, your life changes. The binge becomes a focus of your energies. You may find yourself thinking about your binge when you first wake up in the morning. You may try to organize all your activities so that a certain amount of time is left free for you to be able to binge. On days when you're particularly bored, tense, angry, or depressed, your urge to binge is often the strongest. You may find that you *need* that binge in order to move from one aspect of your day to another, such as from school to home life or to mark the transition from work to relaxation. You'll probably experience feelings of tension and anxiety, perhaps have heart palpitations and break into a sweat right before you actually begin a binge. It's important to recognize these physical sensations. Your body is telling you that you're in a pre-binge state. Those sensations are a signal that you need to take stock of who and what you're reacting to, to assess whether there's someone or something you may be trying to avoid. It's time to remind yourself that if you flip into your binge, you're hiding something from yourself.

What do you do during a binge? Whatever you're eating — whether it's sugary, starchy foods or those that are relatively high in fats, whether it includes "healthy" foods like veggies or is purely "junk," you'll consume a large number of calories. One estimate is that an average binge ranges between 1,200 and 11,500 calories per binge; another estimate asserts that in a large binge, food intake can reach 166 calories per minute. You may use "markers" when you start a binge — foods that have intense colors and are not immediately digestible, such as red apple skins, lettuce, licorice, or drinks such as tomato juice or purple grape juice — so that you can recognize them when you later vomit and know that all you've eaten is purged. The actual eating of the food during a binge is often mechanical — chew, swallow, chew, swallow. There's no effort to taste or savor the food, and no attention is paid to your stomach telling you it's full. You may not even be hungry when you start out. In fact, you'll probably lose the ability to read your body's hunger-satiation signals, and you'll have to relearn this after you stop being bulimic. Bingeing continues until there's no more food left to eat, until the pain caused by ingesting so much food is too much to bear, or until there's an outside interruption (a phone call, a doorbell ringing, a dog barking, someone coming in on you) that breaks your concentration on the food.

Next comes the purge. Purging gets easier the more you do it. Experienced vomiters can contract their diaphragms and abdominal muscles, thereby forcing whatever's in their stomachs into their esophagi and making it easy to vomit. You may take laxatives, diet pills, or diuretics (also called water pills, designed to make you urinate a lot), or emetics (designed to make you vomit) immediately after a binge. But people who rely on laxatives or who take emetics like ipecac find that they need to take more and more as the bulimia continues to get the same effect as the laxatives had at first — which is just what happens if you're addicted to alcohol or drugs.

Bingeing followed by purging is extremely dangerous to your physical health. In the most extreme instances, vomiting can cause your stomach to rupture (burst open). It can cause something called alkalosis, which involves chemical changes in your blood that can then lead to a loss of calcium in your system, as well as tingling in your fingers, tetany (a series of muscle spasms), and damage to your liver, lungs, and heart. It also can burn your esophagus and cause scar tissue to form. Vomiting, because of acid in your stomach, can destroy the enamel of your teeth. Laxative abuse can destroy your bowel function and leave you with perpetual diarrhea and rectal bleeding. It can also wash out the sodium and potassium levels in your system (which diuretics do too), which can cause your heart to beat irregularly. In extreme cases, it can lead to heart failure, which can kill you. If you're female, bulimia can cause menstrual irregularity and may affect your future ability to conceive and bear children. Taking emetics like ipecac is literally putting poison into your body, and you know that poison can kill.

During a binge you may feel free and less tense, but by the end of a binge and with the purging that easing of tension can give way to feelings of guilt about what you've done. They, in turn, will lead to more tension, which makes the conditions right for the whole cycle to begin again.

When you are bulimic your relationship with food changes. It becomes like a narcotic to you. You can't resist certain foods, especially the things we call junk foods. (Most bulimics don't binge on vegetables, chicken, or red meats.) That makes it very hard for you to do ordinary things like going shopping in a grocery store or a bakery. You lose self-control and spend much more money than you should. You may find it hard to get through the checkout lines without eating what you're buying. You may go from place to place repeating the buy-eat pattern until you have enough in your grocery bag to make it look like your shopping trip was a normal one. Bulimia makes you afraid to eat at home or in restaurants with your family or friends because you no longer have confidence in your ability to control your urge to binge, or you can no longer eat anything, even if it isn't during a binge, without purging immediately after.

Bulimia affects you physically, alters the focus of your personality, and also changes how other people relate and react to you. The purging is something that turns other people off. You may find that they were willing to overlook or make excuses for your overeating or junking out, but once you start excusing yourself from the table and come back looking washed out or smelling of vomit, the social nature of sharing meals changes. Your presence is no longer desired. You feel like an outcast, and you may actually find others — even your own family — avoiding you.

Things at home (or school if you live away from home) can go from bad to worse. Once your purging starts impinging on the family turf — the bathrooms reek, the toilets aren't clean, the bed linens get soiled if you lose bowel control or vomit in the wrong place, the food you're hoarding under the beds and in closets starts to spoil or brings in insects, you may even start stealing to support your food habit — you can lose the sympathy of your family or roommates, and you spark tremendous anger. They may not understand why you're doing these things, and they may be frightened when they see that you're out of control.

> Marilyn had been my roommate since we started boarding
> school in ninth grade. By the middle of our junior year
> she'd become like a stranger to me. She started pilfering
> small amounts of money from my purse, thinking I didn't
> notice, and then she snitched my silver ring. Her appear-
> ance got sloppier around mid-semester and she had a body
> odor I couldn't pinpoint. I could feel a kind of rage inside
> me almost every morning, and she seemed totally unaware
> of how I was feeling about her. I didn't have the nerve to
> confront her. It was only when I caught her vomiting and
> saw she had also downed a whole box of Ex-Lax in the bath-
> room that I put two and two together. I got our house-
> mother, who called her parents. Marilyn hates me for it.
>
> *Pammy K., age seventeen*

Because you don't look ill the way an anorectic would, chances are that you'll get tougher treatment from your family than you would if you were emaciated and looked like you were wasting away. If you steadfastly refuse to try to change, or if you're so far enmeshed in the bulimic patterns that you can't make changes on your own, without professional help, people may misinterpret your actions as a slap in their faces, as your attempt to hurt them purposely. Very often, families who try to make sense of the bulimia without fully understanding what's happening end up involved in some domestic violence, as if that would help you "come to your senses." You may find that you're actually being slapped around or verbally abused, you may be subjected to threats about being thrown out of the house, there can be a lot of angry yelling and attempts to assign blame, and often a bulimic family member is told to leave home and stay somewhere else.

> Now that I'm better, I can feel for my parents. I guess they really had no other option but to throw me out. I was destroying our family life. I'd vomit each time I ate anything, and I couldn't hide what I was doing from my little sister. She got so scared of me that she refused to sit in the same room with me alone. Her teacher told my mom that my sister's schoolwork was going downhill. I guess I was the cause. My mom and dad fought over me all the time. It was like living in hell. I left and got picked up by a juvenile officer. That's what brought me into therapy. Thank goodness it worked.
>
> *Yolanda B., age eighteen*

It's very hard to be bulimic — the physical and emotional tolls are tremendous. It's also difficult *not* to be bulimic once you've fallen into the binge-purge habit. But it can be done, and it's worth a try.

Can You Fight Bulimia and Win?

The answer is "yes." Ideally, you'll try to get help from a health care professional, who can be your guide and also your family's guide through the maze of the eating disorder. But even if you don't have immediate access to such a person, there are a few things you can do immediately to start regaining control of your binge-purge urges and to put food back into its proper context.

1. Analyze what Drs. Joel Yager and Carole Edelstein (in an article in *A Comprehensive Approach to the Treatment of Normal Weight Bulimia*) call the "ABCs" of your bulimic symptoms — the *antecedents* (what happens before a bulimic episode), the *behaviors* (what you actually do), and the *consequences* (what happens, how you feel, how others react, how it affects your daily life). How much planning goes into a binge? Where does your binge take place? With whom do you binge? What do you binge on?

2. For each of the "ABCs" that you uncover, try to make one change that might possibly alter your typical response pattern. Repeat this process again and again until you or your family is able to notice that there is some positive change.

3. Try to get in touch with your feelings. Even if they're angry or negative emotions, try to get them out in the open. It's better to express your feelings than to bury them by being bulimic.

4. Force yourself to eat on a normal, planned schedule. Lock the refrigerator and cabinets between meals if you have to. Don't let yourself skip a meal and don't fast. If you can do this for one day, the next day may be easier. Eventually you may be able to string several binge-purge-free days together in a row and you'll be on your way to escaping the eating-disorder maze.

5. Find alternatives to bingeing. Get yourself out of the house at the time you'd normally binge. Go to a place where no food's available. Take a course at night school, go swimming, run a mile at the track, donate your time

to a charity, get an after-school job (not food-related).

6. Understand that you may still want to binge and purge even if you think you've got the bulimia licked. You may find yourself thinking about food even if you don't act on your impulses. Don't get discouraged if this happens.

7. Share what you've learned about bulimia with your family and friends. Working together to achieve a common goal — your health — can be a terrific experience for all of you, even if it's the toughest thing any of you have ever tried.

8. Until you're back in control of your eating habits and understand at least some of the emotional reasons for your bulimia, stay away from people who may have encouraged you to binge (and even purge) with them in the past. Misery does love company, and unfortunately, a lot of kids are enticed by others who function as bulimia pushers and binge buddies.

PART 2

EATING DISORDERS EXPOSED

5
WHEN YOU'RE READY TO CONFRONT THE ENEMY

Fighting Back

When I couldn't deny anymore that I really did have a problem with a name, an *eating disorder*, I couldn't hold back my tears. It was so hard to admit. I didn't want that label. I was mad that I was found out. Sometimes I want help, while at other times I think I'm in control of everything I do. Many times I think that if I tried to get help, I really wouldn't make it, because many times I've tried very hard to stop on my own, but after a couple of days, my mind drives me crazy. I don't think I'm ready to stop yet. (At least that's what my mind tells me.)

But I know I can't live like this. Because I'll either die of malnutrition or my mind will finish destroying me.

Della J., age fifteen

The first step in fighting an eating disorder is admitting to it. That's not as simple as it sounds. It means you have to be willing to develop a level of self-awareness that will let you try to figure out why things have reached the state they're in right now. It's also helpful to have basic knowledge about eating disorders so that you can describe the situation accurately. Reading *When Food's a Foe* up to this point has given you that capability.

It's one thing to read about eating disorders and understand them on an intellectual level; it's another to be able to apply that information to yourself and take action to combat a problem. That can be scary, difficult, and emotionally painful. On the other hand, it can be exciting — almost like going on a quest for the solution to a baffling puzzle, with the potential payoffs being your restored health and happiness. Now it's time to take some steps on the path leading to those positive payoffs.

Nipping Problems in the Bud: Prevention after the Fact

> I grew up with a grandmother who was a walking quote factory. One of her favorites was "An ounce of prevention is worth a pound of cure." I never understood how right that could be until I became bulimic. If I'd had enough smarts to know how to keep myself from bingeing and vomiting I wouldn't have to be talking to you right now, and I'd have saved my family the $2,000 it cost to have my teeth repaired from the acid damage I did by throwing up all the time. I wish I could take back those years.
>
> *Arleine B., age nineteen*

It's easy to admit mistakes once they're over and done with, but it is much more difficult to prevent them from occurring in the first place. Chapters 3 and 4 list some ways in which people can avoid developing an eating disorder. But you may feel that at this point it is too late for primary prevention.

Fortunately, prevention can mean more than just learning the facts about a subject in order to protect yourself. It also refers to

- what you can do to prevent a problem that's brewing from getting worse,
- the steps you can take to prevent a former problem from recurring,
- what you can do to prevent the continuation of a present problem that's negatively affecting many aspects of your life (for example, health, school or work, family and other relationships).

Preventing something that's *already* part of your routine from worsening requires a more specific strategy. You'll have to be willing to take a close look at the factors that are contributing to the problem, take action to change them, and try a number of different tactics to see which ones work best.

Can eating disorders be prevented? The answer's a definite "yes." But unlike diseases where there's a specific virus or other sort of foreign invader in your system that can be combated with medication, with an eating disorder there's no germ or parasite that you can take aim at with a pill or an inoculation to rid yourself of that invader. It's not always clear why the behaviors that are part of eating disorders become so powerful, but it's safe to say that they serve some purpose or else they wouldn't get repeated. Eating disorders are ways in which people cope with things about themselves and their lives that they're not satisfied with. In this respect, then, they start out as being under a person's control. *Anything that has the possibility of being controlled has the potential to be prevented.* What you'll choose to do will depend on your particular set of circumstances, your goals, the time frame you set for yourself, and even your motives. What works for one person might not work for someone else, and what works at one time for you might not be effective every time that preventive approach is used. That's why developing a preventive strategy isn't a precise science.

You need to be honest with yourself about your motives. Are *you* really interested in prevention possibilities, or are you merely responding to someone else who's on your case, such as a parent or a friend? If you're doing it for someone else, the preventive process may be harder to stick with at first, even though you may end up with good results. Are you doing it out of fear? A sense of adventure? Either way, you'll learn things about yourself that you probably weren't aware of. Also, try to be bluntly honest about your expectations. Are you expecting to reach your goals right off the bat, or are you doing it with the understanding that you may fail and have to start from square one again? Can you handle the probability that feelings and situations that you hadn't anticipated will emerge?

So, there's no magic preventive formula that will help everyone control or eliminate eating disorders. There's no equivalent of Contac cold capsules to dry up the symptoms and make you feel better. To make things worse, since anorexia and bulimia can start out as behaviors that seem "normal" and acceptable in our culture, it can be hard to get motivated to want to prevent eating disorders, especially in their early stages, when they don't seem like a real threat or a real possibility. People with eating disorders often justify their actions with comments like:

- "Everybody diets."
- "Being thin is healthy."
- "If junk food's so bad for you, why doesn't the government recall it?"
- "The more I exercise now, the better the chances I'll prevent osteoporosis later."
- "If laxatives were bad, why would they be sold in supermarkets?"

It is important to avoid "psyching yourself out" in the early stages because that's when prevention is least complicated and frequently most successful. The prevention process can be started at any stage during the course of an eating disorder, however — that's the good part about prevention. Even if you've been hospitalized to get you past a health crisis brought on by the eating disorder, you can start planning how to avoid a replay as long as you understand what's involved in the process of prevention. But someone else can't do it to you or for you. You have to do it for yourself.

It Pays to Develop Self-Awareness

One of the toughest aspects of being a teenager or young adult is wanting everybody to think you've got your act together. This means that you may be trying to look and act like you're in control when you're struggling with questions like "Who am I?" "What do I want to do with my life?" "Does anyone really love me?" "Will I ever find happiness?" "Will I be a success?" "How can I be everything that everyone expects me to be?" and so on. It's hard to maintain a veneer of calm, control, and competence when you're feeling like a spring that's about to be sprung and you're not sure where that spring will land!

Let's assume that instead of examining these pressures and stresses constructively — such as by acknowledging them and talking openly about them with family and friends, and by taking action to make changes — you develop an eating disorder as a shield, a way to avoid having to answer tough questions, to avoid having to admit feeling that you're not a "perfect 10" and neither is your life. You really don't have to go that route! Developing self-awareness is within the realm of possibility of each of us and it also happens to be one of the best ways to prevent an eating disorder from taking over your life. Self-awareness can sap the strength of an eating disorder and eliminate the need for it to exist at all by providing the kinds of insights that you need to answer at least partially such questions about yourself. Then they seem less scary. If they're not scary, they become approachable. It follows that if you can approach these questions you can begin to see ways to change certain patterns in your life, empower yourself and take some control, and learn to take credit where credit is due.

How do you develop self-awareness? You need to take a close, objective look at yourself and your situation. Try to figure out the variables in your life that have had an effect on you and may have propelled you in the direction of developing an eating disorder. If you haven't yet read Chapter 2, do so now; if you have, you may want to review it. In a way you're like an archaeologist at a dig site, uncovering layer upon layer of artifacts of a unique civilization in an attempt to figure out the relationship of one layer to another, how the parts fit together and interacted, how they influenced each other, etc. Think about the following questions, some of which you've been asked to consider in previous chapters:

Do you feel in control of your life in general, and specifically where food and eating are concerned?

– What's your personal habit profile like?

– Are the parts of your self-image at war or in synch?

– Do you have freedom of choice about what you eat at home or is yours a "clean your plate or else" family?

What influences you?

– Are there individuals or groups of people you come in contact with who provoke your urge to binge or strengthen your desire to diet?

- Is there a specific event or situation that occurs repeatedly and that usually comes about prior to your binge or strengthens your resolve to restrict what you eat?
- How do you react to media stories about diets and dieting, exercise, physical attractiveness, sexuality, etc.?
- Do you have any idols or role models who are very thin?
- Do you have a coach, parent, or teacher who has pushed you to become thin?
- Do you have any friends who are into dieting or bingeing and purging?

What do you believe?

- Do you believe that losing weight is the way to improve yourself?
- Do you believe that losing weight and being thin are shortcuts to happiness?
- Do you believe that food is the equivalent of love and caring?
- Do you believe that serving and eating food is a way to control others?

What's your typical communication style?

- Do you keep things to yourself, or speak your mind with ease?
- Do you like to fight fair and win, or do you prefer to negotiate?
- Do you give in easily even if you really think you're right?

What do you do in your spare time?

- Do you participate in a sport or other activity (such as ballet) for which a certain low weight is required?
- Do you like doing things alone more than you like doing things as part of a group?

Is there a particular time of day when you're most in need of a binge or when the idea of eating is most threatening?
Write out your answers in as much detail as possible on a separate sheet of paper. By thinking about these issues you focus your attention on influences that you may have over-looked, forgotten about, or refused to acknowledge up to now. The more you explore such questions, the likelier it is that you'll begin to see reasons why you have certain feelings about food and why you behave in certain ways around food. Once you develop this self-awareness you can create a strategy to deal with each influence that fans the flames of the eating disorder and, we hope, extinguish them one by one.

cathy®   **by Cathy Guisewite**

CATHY
COPYRIGHT 1986 UNIVERSAL PRESS SYNDICATE.
Reprinted with permission. All rights reserved.

Taking Inventory of What You've Learned about Yourself

Keeping track of your answers to so many and such complicated questions can be overwhelming. To avoid confusion and to increase your self-awareness, develop a "personal inventory." This is a no-nonsense way of finding out what makes you tick. It's like being a buyer for a store and knowing what's in stock and what's out of stock, what's good for the store and what's bad for it, what should be kept each season and what should be phased out and not reordered.

In your case you're taking inventory of and making decisions about people, things, and situations that have affected your feelings and attitudes about food and eating, and your self-image as well. Make a list of who or what has influenced you up to now, when and where these influences probably began, why you think you paid attention to them, and whether or not you're still under their influence. Be sure to mark with a " + " anything or anyone you think has had a positive impact, and mark with a " − " anything or anyone you think has had a negative impact. You can organize your thoughts in chart form, as shown below.

My Personal Inventory

WHO?	WHEN?	WHAT?	WHERE?	WHY?	STILL?

For instance, your columns might look like this:

WHO?	WHEN?	WHAT? and/or WHERE?	WHY?	STILL?
Mom (+)	always	family dinners	she listens to me	yes, is a help
Dad (−)	always	weekend meals at grandma's	criticizes me, calls me "chub" and watches me eat	yes, even though I'm thin now
Coach (−)	practice	school	says I'm too thin, too weak to be goalie	yes
Ballet teacher (−)	always	class	sets impossible goals for our bodies, I never feel good enough	yes

Boyfriend (+)	always	school and at his house	his house is only place I feel safe eating at, no one watches me, I feel in control there	yes
Best friend (−)	since jr. yr. began	school, at parties	says I'm impossible, is jealous of me	yes
		teen magazines (+, −)	make me wish I looked like a model (−) but teach me a lot (+)	yes

Isolating Your Negative Triggers

I finally realized how much I've resented my mother's insistence on cooking all my meals and sitting with me watching me, expecting me to consume every bite, but I still haven't found the right words to tell her. I'm working on it, though. I'm not going to give her that much power over me. No more. I want to take care of myself. Maybe then I'll be able to enjoy eating again.

Kyle B., age fifteen

My swimming coach spent years telling everyone on the
team to keep our weight down, and he could be counted on
to yell each time anybody gained a few pounds. It got to be
that every time I heard the opening line of his speech,
"Girls, it's apparent you're not serious about the shape you
have to be in . . . ," I got a knot in my stomach and broke
out into cold chills even when the temperature at the pool
was unbearably hot. I'd go home and binge and then have
to vomit every time that happened, and I didn't see the
connection until recently.

Bettina H., age seventeen

My entire eighth-grade year I would get panicky every time
I was asked to go for fries and a Coke after school. I was
afraid to say yes because I didn't want to blimp out, and I
was afraid to say no because I didn't want to lose friends. I
wish I'd been able to go and just have fun. It wasn't my
thing to buck the crowd because I couldn't stand up for myself then. I really wasted a lot of energy worrying about that
stuff and feeling ugly and out of control. I'd go and hate myself. Once I started really dieting I had a legit excuse not to
go. The sad part is now I really am out of control, but I
wasn't then.

Pattie N., age fifteen

I think my eating disorder did originate at home from my
parents. But it wasn't that they *wanted* me to eat or "clean
my plate." No, in our house my mother is a health fanatic
and trying to make substitute low-calorie foods. I thought it
would be *wonderful* to have been in a family that *wanted*
me to eat. I was embarrassed to be hungry in my house and
I knew my mother really wanted me to diet. I felt my parents watching how much exactly I ate, and the pressure
started there. Good people don't eat. Anything else is
shameful.

Janine K., age eighteen

Your personal inventory should give you a pretty clear picture of the elements that have been instrumental in making an eating disorder part of your life. They're probably the items you marked with " − " signs. Now it's time to look at another layer of that imaginary archaeological dig site and expose your *negative triggers:* specific little things that in themselves may appear insignificant but that consistently make you miserable, anxious, uncomfortable, and unhappy and make you turn to anorexia and/or bulimia as your solution or your escape. They're called "triggers" because they operate like the trigger on a pistol: a trigger must be activated before the bullet can be shot and do any damage. So it is with eating disorder triggers: once they're activated, anorectic or bulimic behaviors get released and can do damage.

These negative triggers can take many forms. Usually there is more than one at work. In Kyle's case it was a combination of his mother's insistence on cooking his meals and sitting with him at certain mealtimes; in Pattie's case it was the situation of going to an after-school hangout to eat; in Bettina's case it was a specific line of a coach's speech. Janine wanted to eat but felt she wasn't allowed to be hungry and thought she was being watched as she ate. Negative triggers can be words that are said to you, looks people give you, situations you dislike being in.

Your perceptions of something or someone as negative may not reflect what was actually intended — Kyle's mother didn't mean to drive him nuts; she thought what she was doing for him was motherly and loving. Pattie's friends weren't aware of the conflict raging inside Pattie and actually thought they were all having a good time. Bettina's coach was only trying to get his team into the best shape possible, though he was more than a little dense about how he was coming across. When, as in these cases, the other people's intentions and motivations aren't clear, what's said and done can function as negative triggers that catapult you into eating-disorder patterns. But once the triggers are exposed, they become understandable and more manageable.

How do you isolate your personal negative triggers so you can do something about them? Start by going over the answers to the questions posed in the self-awareness section of this chapter and look over your personal inventory. Try to break things down into their smaller parts. Remember the mathematical rule: the whole is equal to the sum of its parts. You're working backward from the whole (the situation you're in now, either having an eating disorder or feeling very vulnerable to one) to the parts (the triggers) so that eventually you can change the parts and alter the whole!

Write out your answers to the following questions on a separate sheet of paper:

1. What kinds of things that are said to me or about me make me feel bad?

2. What kinds of things that are said to me or about me make me feel good?

3. When I'm in a situation that makes me feel bad or uncomfortable, who or what specifically in the situation triggers the most intense bad feelings?

4. When I'm in a situation that makes me feel great, who or what specifically in the situation triggers the most intense pleasurable feelings?

5. Are there any particular times of the day, week, month, or year when I want to turn to eating-disordered behaviors to make myself able to cope?

6. Are there any particular times of the day, week, month, year when I resist doing what the eating disorder dictates or am turned off at the thought of doing it?

7. When and in what situations am I happiest?

8. When and in what situations am I least content?

9. How do I define "control"?

10. How does an eating disorder function in my life?
11. What does an eating disorder do for me?
12. What does an eating disorder do to me?

Based on your answers to these questions and any others you find yourself thinking about, list your negative triggers.

Negative triggers are totally personal, although many people may have similar triggers. You should concern yourself only with the things that you believe are problematic for *you*, especially if you're in the habit of comparing notes with other anorectics and bulimics, or if your friends and relatives like to spend time telling you what your problems are. Trust yourself. There's no "right" number, no "minimum" number of triggers you need to expose in order to say you're opting for prevention. This isn't a contest in which more is better. In other words, don't "program" yourself to feel inadequate before you get started. You're doing well if you expose just one negative trigger and try to do something to prevent it from operating in the future. If you can pinpoint a problem and describe it clearly, it's probable that you can find a more constructive way to deal with it than by using an eating disorder as your solution. That's why it can be preventive.

Once you expose the triggers you can anticipate them, control them, and prevent them from bursting forth and catapulting you into an eating disorder or keeping you trapped in one. Just remember the concept of cause-and-effect. Your goal is to recognize the cause and change the effect. Doing so can be a hit-or-miss business, but it's worth a try — several tries. Take it one step at a time and don't expect miracles right off the bat.

Here's an example of how the process works.

Fifteen-year-old Anne V.'s best friend, Melinda Z. (age fifteen), had been pressuring Anne to spend a lot of money on clothes and makeup, to exercise with her, and to diet when she wanted to diet. Anne didn't have the free cash to spend that Melinda did, wasn't built like Melinda, and didn't need to exercise in the same way. To make matters worse, Anne wasn't losing weight as fast as Melinda. Anne began feeling pretty down on herself and had been bingeing and using laxatives frequently to relieve both tension and hunger.

After isolating the negative triggers in this situation, Anne devised a strategy. She decided on the following possibilities:

– she could tell Melinda to take her diet and exercise plan and shove it;

– she could say, "I'll be happy to support you but I won't be your clone and I can't follow your program anymore";

– she could say, "What you're asking of me is selfish and you're not taking my needs into account. Here's a list of what I can handle and what I can't. Look it over and then let's talk about some compromises we can make without putting our friendship on the rocks."

Anne tried the last one first, and, luckily, it worked. Her urge to binge and purge lessened almost immediately and she got it under control within three weeks.

Making a personal inventory and isolating your negative triggers won't necessarily cure you or eliminate the need for professional help (psychotherapy or self-help, for example, which will be discussed in Chapter 7) to lead you out of the eating-disorder maze. What it will do is buy you time to think, give you a focus for discussing problem areas with the people who are part of the problem, and increase your ability to exert some control by getting actively involved in confronting and solving what you perceive to be a potential or actual problem.

Defusing Your Eating Environment
One Step at a Time

Now it's time to focus on food and the act of eating. With anorexia and bulimia, the bottom line is to eat or not to eat, how much to eat, and what to do with what's been eaten. Then come the issues of how to handle the feelings that eating or not eating cause in yourself and others, when and why food's a negative force in your life, and how to prevent the focus on food from being destructive.

Defusing your eating environment one step at a time is the next logical step after you've gone to the trouble of isolating your negative triggers. Again, this has to be a very individualized, personal exercise because no two people are alike, and also because what you'll choose to do if you're anorectic is likely to be different from what you'll choose to do if you're bulimic. But one question everyone should answer is "What can I tolerate and what can't I tolerate?" That's because we all have limits. If you can describe what or how much you can eat, who you can eat with, and where you can eat before you reach a point when the anorectic or bulimic patterns get triggered, you can establish a baseline — like a safety zone — that you can try to duplicate each time you face the necessity of dealing with food. Then you can build on the baseline and extend it gradually.

Try to think very logically and analytically about the food that you either eat or don't eat, the food that pleases you or makes you panic, the food that you can keep down and the food that you need to purge from your body. You have the power to make preventive changes.

Does the odor of a particular food or combination of foods play any part in your eating disorder?

If it does, try to change that. Experiment with different foods, keeping in mind the necessity of a balanced diet for health reasons. Wear a noseclip if you have to, to get you past the hurdle of smelling the foods you'll be chewing and swallowing. Spray an air freshener in the area you'll be dining in to mask the food odors. Be inventive and creative, even if you look eccentric or silly in the process. You won't have to do it forever if the tactic works. The idea is that you're trying to defuse that negative trigger, which in this case is food *odor*, and to set up a new series of responses to that trigger that aren't anorectic or bulimic responses.

Does the visual impact of food or combination of foods play any part in your eating disorder?

Some people can't stand to look at meats; others need to organize their foods in particular patterns on a plate; some can tolerate only tiny amounts on a plate at any one time. Again, try to change the power that food on the plate has over you. Experiment. Pretend you're an artist working on a canvas. Change things around till you find a food or combination of foods that won't cause you to flip into your anorectic or bulimic patterns. If you can really get into the mind game of imagining yourself as an artist and the food your medium, you might be able to distract yourself enough so that some of the emotional punch associated with the food may evaporate and you may be able to eat it normally.

Does the taste of any particular food or combination of foods play any part in your eating disorder?

Everybody has preferences for certain kinds of foods, and it's a fact that some foods trigger more intense reactions than others. Problems can occur when you don't have the chance to let your personal sense of taste influence what you eat. Have people in your family always eaten their food cooked with certain spices or to a certain degree of doneness and given you no choice in the matter? Are you particularly sensitive to sweet, salt, sour, or bitter tastes? Do you have food allergies? Do certain tastes make you lose control and throw you into a binge? Do certain tastes repulse you and make it impossible for you to eat anything at all? It's useful to explore these sorts of questions because substituting similarly nutritious foods for the ones you can't stand may be a very simple and effective way of preventing an eating disorder from developing or dominating your life. If you don't know much about foods and nutrition, you can go to a public library and ask the librarian for help in locating appropriate books. Remember that educating yourself is a major part of the preventive process.

Now consider other aspects of the eating environment.

Does the location of the meal play any part in your eating disorder?

It's possible that you can eat in a relatively normal fashion in one location but not in another. Find the location where you can eat relatively normally. Even if that location is the backyard of your parents' house under your favorite tree, start there. However, the key words here are *relatively normal*. We're not talking about finding alternative places where you can feel comfortable *bingeing*. Many bulimics, for example, have no trouble bingeing in their kitchens or stuffing themselves in their bedrooms. Your task is to find the places where you can eat without experiencing the tensions and then flipping into the behaviors associated with anorexia and/or bulimia. Explain to your family what you're doing and why. Don't wait for their permission or their approval. This may seem like an unorthodox suggestion, but if it can relax you enough to eat a meal and *not* get out of control, you can then build your confidence from there. The idea is to get yourself back into the mainstream of being able to eat with family and friends *anywhere,* and to do that you have to start somewhere if an eating disorder is putting barriers in your way.

Do you have any habits/rituals before, during, or after meals that play a part in your eating disorder?

Rituals are a very big part of the life of anorectics and bulimics. Whether the habit is preparing the foods of a binge so that they sit in a certain order on the table, setting up an actual barrier between yourself and whomever else you're eating with so they can't watch you eat, or cutting a single pea into tiny slivers, such habits and rituals should be eliminated. They isolate you by making you focus a lot of energy and attention on the whole eating process, and it's energy that could better be used elsewhere — such as in communicating with people you care about, doing things that are fun for you, learning. A few words of caution, though: don't try to eliminate everything of this nature at once. Again, take it one step at a time. If you have to cut your food in pieces, try to cut fewer pieces. If you have to isolate yourself, set a kitchen timer and give yourself a few minutes before you have to join the rest of the family. Gradually, decrease your time alone. Buy fewer items for the binge. As the preventive tactics start to work, you'll find that your rituals aren't as necessary as you think.

Are there any habits/rituals that other people you eat with frequently engage in before, during, or after meals that play a part in your eating disorder?

Perhaps your grandmother who lives with you belches loudly during meals as a way of showing her satisfaction. You think it's gross. Perhaps before and after dinner your father insists on smoking a smelly cigar that rattles your taste buds and your sense of smell. Your little brother chews with his mouth wide open and seems to do it just to annoy you. Maybe your mother won't sit down to eat until everyone else has sat and spends the time she should be dining with you doing dishes and grumbling about it. Mealtimes are filled with tension as a result. Things of this sort can be eating-disorder triggers. You might want to discuss your reactions with whoever's involved, but this can be hard, especially if it's an older person who might take offense. Another way is to try to understand why things are as they are. Try to develop a sense of humor about it. See if you can suggest alternatives. Negotiate. Even if things don't change to your liking, any positive attempt you make to bring your feelings out in the open is a way of developing control and can be preventive.

Do you have any recurring fears or fantasies about certain foods or combinations of foods that play a part in your eating disorder?

You may worry about a food's effect on you. You may have inaccurate notions about what will happen if you allow yourself to eat certain foods — you'll instantly put on weight all over; you'll develop only fat thighs; your face will get bloated; you'll start a binge; people will think you're weak-willed. Perhaps you've developed a system of "safe" and "unsafe" foods that enable you to get through mealtimes and feel OK about yourself, but the foods that are "safe" aren't balanced and don't provide you with enough calories and nutrients to keep you healthy.

An easy way of determining what you really think and feel about foods is to develop a *food hierarchy.* All you need to do is divide a piece of notebook paper into four horizontal sections starting at the top with one labeled *Safest Foods* (or *Least Forbidden Foods*), then *Somewhat Forbidden Foods,*

Extremely Forbidden Foods, and *Unsafe Foods* (or *Most For-bidden Foods*) as the bottom section. Then you fill in each one. You may be surprised that the foods you list as unsafe are actually foods that you used to prefer and even ate with pleasure (instead of with guilt or fear) — such as French fries or pizza, fried chicken or chocolate cake. The hierarchy will help you see exactly what you're avoiding and will show you the extent to which you're limiting your food choices. The hierarchy makes you accountable to yourself. Once you've written down the names of the foods and categorized them, it's hard to deny what you've been thinking and how you've been acting regarding your foods.

What do you do with the information? You use the hi-erarchy as you would a road map. Only this map will help you reach the goal of *gradually* relearning to eat foods in reasonable amounts that you've listed in the forbidden cate-gories. Every time you succeed in moving a food up through the hierarchy's ranks so that you can include it among your "Safest Foods," you're that much closer to loosening the bonds of your eating disorder.

It's hard to prevent fears and fantasies completely with-out the help of a therapist, but you can do a few things on your own to see if you can start developing a more realistic and accurate series of thoughts and feelings about food. One is to ask yourself, "What's the worst possible thing that will happen to me if I let myself eat this food?" If there's someone you trust and can confide in, ask that person to answer that same question as it applies to you. You'll see how different your answers may be. Chances are nothing earth shattering will happen. Your personality won't change, your I.Q. won't change, your friends won't leave you, your family won't break up just because you ate something that you believed you shouldn't have. Another approach is to try some relaxation exercises. If you have to eat something that you're uncom-fortable with, try listening to music you like before the meal.

Take a leisurely bath. Go for a walk. Call a friend. Snuggle with your pet. Read a good book. Put yourself into a pleasurable situation so that the good feelings you have can be taken with you when you have to deal with the particular food.

What about the "safe" vs. "unsafe" foods? Reward yourself with a "safe" food for each "unsafe" food you eat. Aim for and work up to balanced nutrition. If you're anorectic, this is a great way to lessen your fear of eating and if you're bulimic, it's a great way to try to get control over the kinds of foods that tend to activate your urge to binge. For example, if popcorn's "safe" and chicken isn't, give yourself a bite of popcorn for every bite of chicken you eat. If vegetables are "safe" but fruited yogurt isn't, take a bite of veggies after each mouthful of yogurt. Doing this can help you get so used to the previously "unsafe" foods that they lose their "unsafe" identity and are no longer negative triggers for you, although it can take quite some time for this to happen and it can look pretty odd as you're doing it.

This discussion should give you an idea of how to go about defusing your eating environment one step at a time by altering the negative triggers. Obviously, the topic is so broad that it's not possible in the space of one chapter to cover all that might apply to your situation. You know yourself best and you can decide what needs to be worked on. You have the power to implement changes that will improve the quality of your life. But be aware that changes can be scary. There's the element of the unknown: will the changes work? Will I be better off? What will the ripple effect be on my family and friends? Will I be able to concentrate on anything other than food and eating? What if I fail? What if I try to prevent the wrong things?

Wondering about these sorts of things is natural, but it's unnecessary. Prevention doesn't demand perfection.

Prevention is possibilities. It's control that frees you to pick
and choose the things you want to change as well as the people
you want involved in the change. Prevention is learning
enough about yourself to develop a safe and healthy life-style
instead of living as a pawn in an eating-disordered one.

A Blueprint for Positives

Another helpful step is to develop a blueprint for the life you
can lead with eating disorders either eliminated or in check.
Here are some guidelines.

1. Don't try to build a castle before you've had the chance to build a hut.

This means that your blueprint should start out simple.
Pick out one or two tasks to defuse the negative triggers *you*
really want to work on and think you can conquer — eating
one meal per weekend with the family without giving in to
the urge to binge or restrict what you eat, controlling what
you buy in preparation for a binge, explaining to your mother
that something she says makes you very uncomfortable and
is part of your problem with eating, for example — and keep
trying to accomplish them until they don't trigger an eating
disordered response anymore. Limiting yourself this way will
help you develop the skills and self-confidence to undertake
more complicated tasks and reach your goals.

2. Get into the habit of revising your blueprint every four to six weeks.

You want to give yourself a reasonable time period in
which to try your preventive strategies that isn't too short or
too long. This way if things aren't going well and don't click,
you can reset your goals and strategies and start fresh without
getting frustrated; if things *are* going very well, you'll have a

sense of accomplishment and can turn your attention to other goals that will also help prevent your being victimized by an eating disorder.

3. Every architect has colleagues. Decide who yours will be and establish ground rules for your relationship.

Don't try to create this blueprint and work from it alone. Think ahead of time about people you'd feel comfortable getting involved with and who would really be able to help you. Eventually, you'll want to "come out" with your secret and ask for help. They can be the people who are part of your problem. They can be people who aren't but are willing to be your sounding board and who'll answer your question "How am I doing?" You might want to tell a lot of people what you're trying to accomplish or just a few. The key is to be prepared to have someone to talk with as you try your preventive strategies, because another person's perspective is always useful even if it doesn't happen to agree with yours.

Another key is to think about the ground rules you'll want for your relationship. Do you want the other person to initiate a discussion of how things are coming along, or do you want to be the one to do this? Are you willing to discuss things at any time, or do you prefer a certain time of day or night? Do you want to be informal about things or do you want to actually make appointments for these discussions? Can you agree to disagree? Setting ground rules like this after you've actually made contact with your helping person can let you develop the sense of control so necessary in preventing an eating disorder at any stage of its development.

A final word about ground rules that might be hard for you to accept right now. If you have hung out with so-called friends who have functioned as your binge buddies, who have acted as diet demons and encouraged you to diet excessively, or who have been bulimia pushers, pressuring you to entice others to try what you've all been doing with food, *you must change the rules of those relationships* if you wish to stay friends with them. In practical terms, that means you have to tell them, "I'm not doing any binges with you from now on and don't try to change my mind" or "I don't want to talk about or try the latest laxatives and diet drinks or diet pills anymore" or "I'm not going to compare our weights each morning with you guys" — and tell them why. Friends who care about you and are interested in helping you regain your health will try to accommodate you. But if they seem angry or try to make you feel that you're being unreasonable, *don't feel guilty* and *don't back down*. Sometimes you have to face up to the fact that such people who masquerade as your friends may be in worse shape than you are. Based on their behavior with you, it's likely that they're eating-disordered individuals who aren't quite ready to acknowledge their own problems and need to surround themselves with like-minded people to make their own behaviors and choices appear ordinary and natural. But once you decide to be the architect of your own recovery and create a blueprint for change, you're in a position to realize that eating-disordered choices and behaviors aren't ordinary and natural — they're dangerous and self-destructive — and you won't be afraid to stick with your new ground rules.

4. Keep a weekly log of how you're progressing.

A weekly log can keep you aware of the things, situations, and behaviors you've been able to change up to now and may not need to keep working on, things you want to continue working on, and those you've been less successful in preventing and need to develop new strategies to work on. You can write it out as a diary with extensive descriptions of what's happened and what you've tried to do about it, or you can write it out as a briefer log with headings like these:

Preventive Task: (describe it) _____
Goal: (describe it) _____
What has to be done to achieve the goal: (list the elements
  involved) _____
Days the task is carried out: (write the actual date) _____
How did it go? _____
Risks: (list them even if you think they're just in your imagi-
  nation) _____
Gains: (list them) _____
Needs further work? ("yes" or "no") _____
Goal achieved? ("yes" or "no") _____

**5. Evaluate your successes at least once during every four-
to six-week period, ideally every week.**

Get into the habit of taking credit for your successes.
Focus on the positives. Talk with the people who are in this
with you and get their opinions of what you've been successful
with. Chances are they'll see more than you do.

This is a lot of work, but it will pay off in the long run
because it will allow you to cope with and change the elements
of your eating environment. Preventive strategies empower
you to remove or control your negative triggers and make
substitutions so you won't find yourself wandering down the
eating-disorder path endlessly and aimlessly.

6

"COMING OUT"

When Your Secret
Is an Eating Disorder

Being honest with yourself, about yourself, can often be difficult, and sharing that honesty with others is even more difficult. It means stripping away many of the protective layers of your personality: your habits, quirks, and eccentricities, your hopes, fears, and fantasies, getting to the barebones core of your identity, and allowing yourself and others to evaluate it. Sometimes that identity doesn't want to be exposed, especially if a big part of it involves doing things that are harmful or self-destructive, or if the choices you make about how you're living your life aren't the choices that the majority of us would make. We all want to keep certain things about ourselves secret, especially things that put us in a bad light. We also try to keep secret anything that would make us feel threatened, insecure, or embarrassed if brought out into the open.

Having an eating disorder and allowing yourself to be ruled by it is the kind of secret that you probably want to keep private. Both anorexia nervosa and bulimia put layer upon layer of those self-destructive habits into your life-style (though you don't usually see it that way when you're really into those behaviors). The more of these layers that fall into place, the more you tend to hide them from the awareness of other people. The more secretive you become about your life-style, the more you can get lulled into the false belief that anorexia and bulimia are secrets that *can* be hidden indefinitely. They're not.

When Other People Try to Get You to Give Up Your Eating Disorder

Eventually, eating disorders creep into other people's awareness because the symptoms are so dramatic, triggering intense responses: people worry about you, feel scared by your actions, and can be unsure how to react to you. But react they do, out of concern and caring for you, and also out of frustration. They often end up wanting to correct or cure your eating disorder without really knowing how.

A battleground mentality sets in. The eating disorder is the ENEMY, you are its VICTIM, and the other person (for example, a parent, friend, relative, or teacher) becomes your RESCUER. Typically, several people will confront you about your eating habits (even if they don't know specifically that what you have is an eating disorder and don't use technically correct terms to describe what they think you're doing), so it's possible to have many would-be rescuers. You may hear, "You're too thin," or "You're not taking care of yourself. You should pay more attention to what you're doing to yourself." People who are aware of the symptoms and consequences of eating disorders may try to use logic and present you with the facts about the dangers to your physical and mental health. When those arguments don't get the desired changes in your behavior, rescuers may try to shake you up with threats of dire consequences: "You'll lose all your friends"; "You won't be allowed to continue living with us if you keep this up";

"You'll have to be sent to the hospital." Sometimes they try the guilt-trip technique: "Look what you're doing to us"; "If you cared about anyone else, you wouldn't do this." Sometimes they abandon the logical approach, get emotional, and beg you to stop what you're doing to yourself.

If you're not ready to accept that help, if you feel protected by your eating disorder and have no interest in listening to the other person's point of view no matter how logical it supposedly is, any attempts at changing your mind can feel like a power struggle, with one person trying to take control and the other feeling powerless. The balance of power between you can shift back and forth and may even accomplish something your rescuer didn't have in mind: the power of your eating disorder can get stronger. That's because pressure from the outside to change something that is such an important part of your identity can make you feel threatened and frightened. Consciously or unconsciously, you may become more stubborn in your resolve to keep things going exactly as they are in your life to avoid feeling scared.

> I've always wanted to reach the stage of being truly anorectic, but I couldn't reach my goal because my parents interfered. They ruined it. They made me go to a shrink and I was furious because I wimped out and didn't get to the point where the anorexia was totally noticeable. But then I overheard my parents talking and they mentioned the doctor had said I wasn't that bad. So I thought, *Well, I'll show them — I'll get there.*
>
> *Felicity L., age sixteen*

Trying to keep your rescuers at bay and at least part of your "secret" unexposed may lead to some very frustrating conversations that are emotionally draining, partly because they are based on your lies about your behavior. The following responses are typical of things said by anorectics and bulimics who *aren't* ready to give up their eating disorders.

Reply #1: *"That's definitely not me."*

This is a way of saying to others that they're misinterpreting your behavior. Unfortunately, it's usually not true and it won't necessarily get rescuers off your trail. It's a response that may be interpreted as your unwillingness to face up to reality; your denial often brings about stronger efforts from whoever is confronting you, in order to get you to admit to the seriousness of your situation.

Reply #2: *"Everybody does it."*

This is the safety-in-numbers, lemming response. There may be a grain of truth in your statement: many people do diet to extremes, and bingeing and purging is fairly common among certain groups of athletes and college students, but "everybody" does *not* do it! This reply is not sufficient to get people who don't share your obsessions and compulsions to believe that your behavioral choices are the norms in our society.

Reply #3: *"It's part of my routine. I do it for me. It's my choice. It's no different from choosing to wear deodorant or not."*

A rationalization of this sort is a way of showing that you have free will and your eating or dieting behavior is voluntary. It's also an attempt to trivialize the importance of an eating disorder in your day-to-day life. The trouble is that if you have to deny and trivialize what's obvious to everyone else, the eating disorder is not a matter of free will and free choice at all, but a habit that is out of control, now in control of you.

Reply #4: *"I have to do it to . . ."* (*make the team, make the weight class, keep in shape, feel good, be happy*).

With statements like these you attempt to make it seem like there's perfect logic behind your behavior, a method to your madness. What remains unsaid is the impact the method has on your health. Such a reply invites the other person to bombard you with facts, facts, and more facts to disprove your logic.

Reply #5: *"I'm not a druggie, so get off my case."*
This is an angry, confrontational response that tries to minimize the actual seriousness of the eating disorder by calling attention to something worse — addictive, illegal drug-taking behavior — that you're *not* engaged in. Sometimes, though, the person you're replying to will pick up the argument and weave in comparisons to drug addictions, so you may actually add more fuel to that person's fire with your reply.

Reply #6: *"It's none of your business,"* or *"It's my body, my business, my life."*
These are the equivalents of pleading the Fifth, attempts to short-circuit any further conversation. What's more likely to happen, though, is that whoever you're replying to will get angrier and more frustrated with you and will begin talking *at* you rather than trying to reason with you.

Reply #7: *"I'll eat what you cook . . ."(the anorectic's reply)* or *"I'll stop eating so much junk food . . ." (the bulimic's reply) ". . . if you stop watching me like I'm a baby."*
You may have a valid point — it's no fun to have every bite of food you eat monitored by someone else. But the "let's make a deal" tone — "I'll do this if you do that" — is a lie. It's a giveaway that you're just playing games. It would be more honest to say, "Let's lay our cards face up on the table and work out a solution from there," but that will only happen if you're ready to "come out" on your own.

Why "Coming Out" Is Better than Being "Found Out"

If you have an eating disorder and your secret is out or you feel it's about to be out, it's better (though harder) to decide to "come out" of your own free will. To understand what is involved in "coming out," think about how the phrase is used in our language. "Coming out of the closet"refers to revealing something very private and out-of-the-ordinary about yourself, usually about your sexual choices. "Coming out" is also used to describe what young women do when they're presented to society at debutante balls. These are huge parties given by parents who are active in certain social groups so that their daughters can be introduced to the adult members of that same group. Each girl who "comes out" is subjected to intense scrutiny — attention is focused on how she looks and how she behaves, and people at the party decide if she has the stuff to make it as the next generation of that social group. Many girls whose parents would like them to "come out" actually choose not to, for these very reasons.

"Coming out" with the admission that you have an eating disorder has elements of both of these usages. It calls attention to the fact that you're doing something that isn't the norm, isn't what the majority of people do. It also puts you in a situation in which you'll be the subject of intense scrutiny. The difference between "coming out" and being "found out" is that when you "come out" you're taking charge. You're also giving permission for other people to help you deal with your eating disorder. When you "come out" you may not be able to predict what the end result of your decision will be, but at least you aren't fighting your rescuers anymore, so your energies can be focused on getting yourself out of the eating-disorder trap.

Because having anorexia and/or bulimia isolates you from the people and events in your environment, "coming out" may just well be the ultimate act of courage for an anorectic or bulimic. It's a self-revelation that exposes the core of your vulnerability — the eating disorder — and gives other people the opportunity to understand and help. "Coming out" removes the mystique and aura of your secret, and in the light of logic the behaviors involved in anorexia and bulimia can look pretty ugly. It proves you're willing to be in the spotlight, and puts you in the position of being like an actor or actress taking direction from a demanding director: having to listen to someone else, learn things about yourself from that other person, and change your behaviors to fit the director's sense of how you should be acting. The identity of that director will depend partly on how serious your eating disorder's effect has been up to now on your mental and physical health. It could be a doctor, therapist, or nutritionist, or it could be a parent, friend, teacher, or someone who has recovered from an eating disorder. It's possible to have many directors helping you in your effort to conquer an eating disorder. Directors and rescuers can be the very same people; the difference between them is your attitude toward them and what they're trying to do for and with you.

There are no guarantees that "coming out" will be met with applause and praise from the people you "come out" to, but, as the saying goes, "no strain, no pain, no gain." It's natural to have fears, and it's even normal to wonder, "Why bother?" The unknowns are risky and you might feel a little like the mythical Pandora, who opened her box and let out all the ills and evils into her world. In reality, though, the risks can be counterbalanced by the gains, and "coming out" can have a positive impact on your life, especially if you've done some advance planning.

Getting the Most out of "Coming Out"

Making the decision to "come out" may be the hardest thing you've ever done. But once the decision's made, preparing yourself isn't that much different from preparing to take on any other challenge in your life, whether it's taking a big exam, giving a recital, acting in a play, or going on a college or job interview.

To improve the odds that the gains will outweigh the risks of "coming out," you should have some definite goals and a clear idea of how you plan to reach those goals. That means you'll want to think about the impact of the communication process, because when an eating disorder is in control, communication tends to be one-sided or absent; "coming out" is a signal that you're ready to reinstitute two-way communication, and you're probably out of practice. You'd be wise to imagine how you're going to communicate your needs and expectations to others and then think about what it will feel like to have other people bounce their ideas off you without your rejecting them out of hand. Give some thought to the following issues.

What do I hope to accomplish by "coming out," right now and in the long run?

Do you just want to get people off your case, or do you really want help to shake the eating disorder? Are you looking for sympathy, or are you sick of being the object of so much sympathy and attention? Do you want to take an active role in your recovery and do most of the work yourself, or are you more interested in getting other people constructively involved in your life and working with them toward a common goal? Do you want to rekindle old relationships that have been hurt by the eating disorder, break ties with the past, or have old and new relationships blend in a new reality for you?

Who do I want involved with me in this process?

Do you want to involve family and friends right away, or rely first on the help and advice of doctors, therapists, or self-help groups before "coming out" to all the people who were part of your pre-eating disordered life? Do you want a combination of people — professional and family/friends — involved in your quest for health? When you pick a friend to confide in, do you know for sure that the person can handle the responsibility of knowing about your problem? Will he or she keep it in confidence or is there any likelihood that your troubles will be broadcast all over school or the neighborhood? Are you prepared for that possibility? Will you be able to tell your friend what you expect to result from the two of you sharing this information about your eating disorder? If you plan to confide in family members, are you willing to accept the possibility that their reactions may not all be sweetness and light, and can you deal with the possibility that they may say things you really don't want to hear? If you think "coming out" to friends and family may be more stressful than successful — but you want to do it anyway — talk first to a therapist (or a teacher, clergyperson, school nurse, or school counselor), who will help you "come out" to these people.

Where and when will I actually "come out"?

Do you envision a family gathering at which you'll make a formal declaration? Will you "come out" gradually, discussing your eating disorder when it seems appropriate and when you meet up with different people at different times? Will you begin the process of "coming out" only if confronted and asked specifically about your eating habits, or will you volunteer information about your disorder? Will you go to a self-help group and "come out" in the protective environment of that group before telling your family and friends? Will you do it anonymously by calling a hotline or helpline?

What will I want to say when I "come out" and how will I say it?

Will you just want to discuss the facts about your eating behaviors, or will you want to discuss your emotions and motivations as well? Will you be willing to delve into issues of family dynamics one-on-one with your relatives, or will you want a negotiator like a therapist or counselor with you for such discussions? Will you want to accuse, appease, or cajole the people you "come out" to? Will you allow yourself to be angry?

Here are some opening lines you might use in this situation.

- "I'm ready to discuss some things about myself that might make you uncomfortable. I need to know whether you think we can talk without your lecturing or yelling."

- "I have a problem with food. I think you're probably aware of it. I don't know what to do about it and I'd like to hear your ideas. Here's what's going on. . . ."

- "I'm anorectic/I'm bulimic/I'm anorectic sometimes and bulimic sometimes. I can't handle this by myself anymore, and I need some help from you. I'm not sure what kind of help, though, and I want to discuss the possibilities."

- "All the things about me that were worrying you are true. You were right to be concerned. I wasn't ready to hear it before, but I'm willing to talk now. I want you to know I'm a little scared to do this."

- "I don't like what's happening to me anymore. I may not like what you have to say, but I want your opinion about what I should do."

- "I can't guarantee how I'll react when we talk, but I'm tired of all the tension around here. I'm anorectic/I'm bulimic/I'm anorectic and bulimic and I need to know how you feel about that."

If you feel that you can't say these things face-to-face with someone, putting similar thoughts in a letter and asking for a response will probably work.

What will I do if I get criticized?

For instance, will you retreat and refuse to discuss things or will you experience the criticism as part of the challenge you choose to face? Will you turn to someone else — someone you still trust absolutely — to discuss your feelings about being criticized? Will you confront your critics and ask for clarification? Will you be tempted to criticize back as a tit-for-tat thing, or will you try to get them to see your point of view without resorting to playing games? Can dialogue exist when there is criticism?

Another good exercise to maximize the positive effects of "coming out" is to write some scripts. Think about what will happen when you "come out" — who will be involved, where and when it will be, what the dialogue will sound like, and what the end results will be. Do a "worst-case scenario" (a scene in which everything that you would not want to happen does), a "best-case scenario" (a scene in which everything works out perfectly), and an "actual situation scenario" (your idea of what will really happen). Usually, reality falls somewhere between the two extremes, with elements of the best and the worst that you imagine could happen.

Here are two scripts to give you an idea of how they could be done.

Worst-Case Scenario Script

Participants: Mom, Dad, Danny (age eight), Paula (age twelve), Me (Gabby, age sixteen)
Time: After dad gets home from work and before dinner
Place: The family room in our house

Dialogue
Me: "I've decided to be honest about myself with all of you."
Paula: "You couldn't be honest if your life depended on it."
Mom: "Paula, stop it."

Dad: *"This better be important. I have a business meeting later and I need to eat and get out of here fast."*
Danny: *"What's for dinner, what's for dinner?"*
Me: *"Isn't anyone listening to me?"*
Paula: *"Everyone listens to you, Gabby, but you always make us out to be the bad guys and make it seem like you never get paid any attention. Is it about how thin you are? Do you want us to tell you how GREAT you look?"*
Mom: *"Gabby, please, don't get into another argument with your sister. Just talk."*
Me: *"What's the point? You think you know what I'm going to say even before I say it. I don't know why I thought you'd hear me now. I'm going to my room. Don't bother calling me for dinner."*
End Results: *Things stay the same between me and the rest of the family. I'll keep on not eating because I know it gets a rise out of Paula at least. I'll probably get real sick or something, and then they'll start listening to me.*

Best-Case Scenario Script
(Same participants, time, and place as in above script.)

Dialogue
Me: *"I've decided to be honest about myself with all of you."*
Mom and Dad: *"We've been waiting for this for a long time."*
Me: *"I think I'm anorectic."*
Paula: *"We've known that for a while. I've been so worried about you, but you never want to talk. You think I'm just a silly little kid. But I feel for you."*
Mom: *"What do you want us to do? We'd like to try to understand you, but we're afraid to push you too hard. You look so fragile right now."*
Danny: *"When's dinner? I'm hungry."*
Me: *"I'm scared of eating."*
Mom: *"Is it my cooking?"*
Me: *"No, Mom, it's not that. I want to be really thin. I have to be really thin."*
Dad: *"You were fine the way you used to be. You didn't have*

*to make yourself thin. We loved you any way you were; well,
we didn't like your punk phase, but we still loved you even
then. You're smart and cute and nice. . . ."*
Me: *"But you never told me any of this before. You never told
me I was OK, I never knew you approved of me."*
Mom: *"We thought you knew how we felt."*

(*Etc.*)

End Results: *I "hear" my family say things I never heard
before. I feel they're concerned about me and that they love
me but I think they don't understand me yet. A real dialogue
can happen from here. I think they're on my side.*

What will I do if my disclosure leads others to tell me things I'm unprepared or scared to hear?

It's important to admit that you're surprised or a little
scared by what the other person told you and to use that
admission as a launching pad for honest discussion. When the
first edition of *When Food's a Foe* was published, a number
of readers wrote to me about just this dilemma. I'd like to
share a few of their letters with you, to show you the kinds
of problems they faced and to help make it easier for you to
anticipate and handle similar situations.

Unanticipated Situation #1: *Your parent has also had
an eating disorder.*

Dear Nancy,
      There is a concern I have that wasn't mentioned in
your book. When I "came out," my mom confessed that she
has bulimia. . . . This has its good and bad sides. We need
to be there for each other for support, but it's hard because
either we concentrate too much on our own problem or the
other's. It's a delicate situation to live with; she's overpro-
tective and quick tempered, and our arguments are about
food, appearance, and our treatment of each other.

If you could address this dilemma in an upcoming book, I would be very grateful.

Sincerely,
Marla G.

This situation can be ticklish, but it can also lead to incredible discussions and amazing depths of understanding between parent and child. Arguing is a sign that communication is blocked, a signal that you're frustrated and not feeling heard. Instead of arguing, make a contract to "agree to disagree" about certain issues that can't be solved immediately. Acknowledge from the start of any conversation that neither of you can pretend about what's going on. Admit that each of you knows what an eating disorder feels like physically and emotionally and that, as a result, each of you will worry even more than usual about the other. If you think the fact that you share the same problem will lead you to feel more "watched" than you want to be and make privacy seem elusive or impossible to achieve, get that fear out in the open. Talk about what it was like to hear your mom make her admission and tell her if it has made you feel too vulnerable, as if there were an extra set of eyes following you around at all times. It could seem as if you are in a competition with your mom: you may feel as if you have to be perfect from now on about your eating, as if you can never admit to needing to binge or purge again. You may feel super guilty if you ever do have a binge-purge episode and you believe that your parent's eating thoughts and behaviors are in perfect control.

On the other hand, your mother might be just as concerned that you will be in control and she won't. She may be experiencing her own feelings of guilt, not only because she has an eating disorder, but because she believes she is somehow responsible for your becoming a bulimic. Either of you might feel annoyed at the other because people with eating disorders often like to believe that they're unique, as if they've *discovered* the particular eating disorder. It's hard to admit that being bulimic isn't unique; it can be even more difficult when someone in your family figured out how to do it first.

To complicate matters further, you could conclude that you're a clone of your parent, someone without a separate identity. Your discovery that you and your mother are each struggling with an eating disorder may magnify what you don't like about her, obscure what you do, and undermine your confidence in your ability to ever become your own person. You need to talk about all these issues together, and if that seems unsafe or too hard, find a therapist to help you do it.

Unanticipated Situation #2: *Your parent doesn't seem to care that you have an eating disorder.*

Dear Nancy,
    I have been bulimic for almost three years now. I am sixteen and fairly attractive. I keep telling myself that I'm never going to do it again but only end up overeating. After I started puking on a daily basis, I became very depressed and decided to tell my mom so she could help me. When I told my mom, she acted like it wasn't a big deal and told me not to do it anymore. It wasn't that easy. My mom knows I never quit throwing up but she never really says anything. It kinda makes me feel like she doesn't care. . . . I often feel like committing suicide and tell myself that I don't deserve to live.

Sincerely,
Lucia P.

Sometimes parents don't say anything about a child's eating disorder because of fear — fear of offending you, fear of finding out the truth, fear of losing your love, fear of making things worse for you. Sometimes parents don't say anything because they literally don't know what to say. They may not understand what's happening and so don't have the words to talk with you in the way you want and need to be talked to.

Sometimes parents don't speak out because of their own frustration and anger at not being able to stop their child's eating disorder, and they figure that keeping quiet is preferable to saying (or doing) something ugly or destructive.

When you "come out" and tell your family and friends about your eating disorder, you also need to tell those people what you need and expect from them. If you want to talk and you need their help, you must be willing to restate that again and again until you feel that you are being heard. If your parents are still unable to do this for you (and sometimes that is the case), you may just have to make peace with that fact and not fight it. Each of us has to cope with situations in our families that are less than perfect and that we're not directly responsible for. If your family doesn't have the communication skills to make you feel they understand you, that's your particular less-than-perfect situation. Don't blame yourself; don't feel as if there's something wrong with you, that you don't deserve to live. You do deserve to live. You are courageous to have been so honest about yourself, and that courage will help you succeed in overcoming your disorder. There are other people who can give you the validation you seek — teachers, friends' parents, counselors, therapists, friends. You don't have to confront and conquer your eating disorder alone.

Unanticipated Situation #3: *When you tell your boyfriend about your eating disorder, he makes light of your problem.*

Dear Nancy,
  I finally got up the nerve to admit to my boyfriend that I was anorexic and had been seeing a therapist for a month. He acted like it was a joke, and told me he'd been a recovering alcoholic for ten months now — that was a *real* problem — and that he'd been abstinent from liquor since joining Alcoholics Anonymous right when we started dating.
  When I described the kind of therapy I was doing, my

boyfriend said it would never work. He told me the only way to get better was to get involved in a self-help setup like his at Alcoholics Anonymous, and that I was crazy to waste my money on a shrink. He made it sound so cut and dry, like his road to recovery was better than mine — it was like we were playing "dueling therapies" or something.

Now I have doubts about my therapy, and I'm scared that if I choose to stick with it, my boyfriend won't approve so I'll have to keep it a secret. What should I do?

Sincerely,
Sharmayne G.

Recovering from any kind of addictive behavior is not something to compete over. Choosing a type of therapy, a therapist, or a self-help group is an intensely personal matter, and what works for one person might not be appropriate for somebody else. But the "dueling therapies" issue, as Sharmayne so aptly described it, is one that comes up often between partners in relationships. It betrays a common problem that guys, recovering from addictive behaviors or not, have in trying to understand eating disorders. A lot of guys admit that they "just don't get it" when their girlfriends try to explain about anorexia or bulimia. For the most part, guys in our society are brought up to think about body shape and weight differently than girls do. As a result, it can be very hard for guys to empathize with the "thin is in/trim is in" messages girls are taught to believe.

Anyone who would imply that an eating disorder isn't a "real" problem needs to be set straight. A boyfriend like Sharmayne's needs to read articles and books about eating disorders; at the same time, Sharmayne needs to tell him she's willing to read about his problem. Then they can compare and contrast the information they've read about each other's situation.

Whenever "dueling therapies" occurs, it's important to

participate in each other's therapy to better understand what each entails. Then if a spirit of competition still seems to exist between you, it needs to be discussed openly and honestly. Occasionally, a guy will mock his girlfriend's road to recovery because he's trying to maintain the upper hand in a relationship; sometimes it's his way of saying he's scared that in the course of her therapy she might discover she doesn't care for him anymore. Whatever happens, though, secrecy is never an option. Secrecy encourages the maintenance of eating-disordered thoughts and behaviors; being open and honest helps you overcome them. The bottom line is that the only person who has to approve of your therapy is you.

If you're willing to do all the things suggested and discussed in this chapter and in Chapter 5, then it should be obvious to you that you're serious about getting control of your eating disorder and that's great! You're putting yourself in a position to be able to admit that there may be a new reality in store for you, a future that doesn't include an eating disorder to dominate your thoughts and actions. Go for it!

7
WHEN YOU NEED
ADDITIONAL HELP

I'd been dieting for over a year, and I was on the verge of being really sick. The more I dieted, the more I needed to diet. I kept saying I was doing this because I wanted to. I didn't — not then, at least — the dieting was like a demon pushing from inside me and pushing me in all the wrong directions. I guess I was lucky. I met a girl at school who'd done the same thing and she helped me realize I couldn't kick it myself. She'd been there and knew my thoughts. She was like my guide out of a maze.

Penny L., age sixteen

Having an eating disorder *is* like entering a maze alone, without a map or compass, unsure of the location of the exits, and unsure when or if you'll find your way out. Even if you entered that maze voluntarily at first, the longer you're in it the more it confounds and frustrates you as you try to spring free of it. Sometimes it seems easier to give up than to continue searching for the exit.

If you've been anorectic and/or bulimic for some time, you may have reached the point where you're tired of fighting the disorder that's been taking up so much of your energy and has distracted you from getting on with other aspects of your life. You may also be tired of getting into hassles with other people about your odd relationship with food and eating issues. As your anger and frustration with their inability to understand you mount, their anger and frustration with their inability to get you to change also mount. So they may tell you that what you're doing to yourself is "wrong," "dangerous," "crazy," "illogical," "abnormal." It's not that they're looking for a fight or are trying to put you down. The words that they use to describe how they perceive your behavior reflect their own fears — both for you and of you — since what you've chosen to do scares them, and they want you to stop and get back to normal.

Perhaps you've tried to deal with your eating disorder on your own by attempting to take control and avoid giving in to your impulses by using a variety of preventive techniques (see Chapter 5), or by "coming out" (see Chapter 6), but nothing has worked. Time after time you relapse, only to find yourself back in your awful-but-comforting self-destructive patterns. So now you've decided to let the anorexia or bulimia be the dominant force in your life. You don't have the desire to do battle anymore. But if you give up, if you retreat deeper and deeper into your world of obsessions and compulsions, you're giving that eating-disorder maze the opportunity to engulf you and sap your will to get out. Although you may *honestly* see that as your only option, it isn't. The time when you feel the most isolated and alone, when you believe no one else could possibly understand, much less help you, is the time when you need to be helped the most. We aren't meant to live our lives alone, and there's no commandment that says, "Mistakes are forever."

Coming to terms with what you have to do for yourself is easier said than done, however. You must consider another option: that it's possible to find a guide who's capable of leading you out of the eating-disorder maze, and willing to do so.

You may feel that this is a good option as far as other people are concerned, but it may be difficult for you to consider it for yourself. In fact, it takes more courage on your part to choose this route than it does to give in to the power of the eating disorder.

By acknowledging the fact that you can't go it alone anymore, you're making a commitment to allow someone else to help you from now on. And if you're willing to accept help, you may be willing to get involved in some kind of psychotherapy. These may be difficult steps for you to think about and take, but they're positive ones, the kind that will put you in the right direction to get out of the maze. Choosing this option proves you *do* in fact have the ability to exert some self-control over the choices you make in your life and that you're not simply a slave to your impulses and obsessions.

Some Basic Facts about Psychotherapy

You may not know what psychotherapy is (from now on it'll be referred to as therapy, its more popular name) or what to expect from it. Some people hear the term *therapy* and immediately think "shrink." They believe that going into therapy means a psychiatrist will be dictating to them what they should be thinking and how they should be acting. In fact, therapy shouldn't be like that at all. *It should be a partnership between you and whomever you're working with*, whether it's a medical doctor, who can attend to your physical problems as well as your psychological stresses (M.D.'s are licensed to prescribe medication for you, and if you have physical problems either caused by or made worse by an eating disorder, your therapist will probably be an M.D. by necessity), or whether it's a trained social worker or psychologist, who can help you deal with your psychological problems but can't prescribe medicines, or whether it's a team of these people.

Therapy is a two-way street: the therapist listens to you and makes suggestions about how you can improve things in your life, you listen to the therapist and respond to those suggestions, and *together* you come to an accurate understanding of your situation and what's best for you. This is sometimes an uncomfortable process, if what the therapist has to say isn't what you want to hear, but — as with any communication — it gives you the opportunity to grow and change in a positive direction.

Therapy works best when a base of trust exists between the participants in the therapy process. Trust makes it possible for an honest exchange of information. Trust evolves gradually as people get to know one another, and you have to give it time. On the other hand, you shouldn't hesitate to tell your therapist if you feel that trust is lacking, especially during the early stages of therapy. This can be a scary prospect, but it is necessary, because without a trust base, frustrating and counterproductive situations can occur — such as the ones described in the following letters:

Dear Nancy,
    I'm a seventeen-year-old anorexic, 5′6½″ and 92 pounds. . . . I'm supposedly in therapy, but nothing seems to happen there. I only see my counselor once every two weeks — which is definitely not enough. I've tried to bring it up, but I think he hates me. . . .

Sincerely,
Sydney B.

and

Dear Nancy,
    I hope you're not mad because I keep writing to you, but my life is OVER! I told my therapist how I felt about not getting anywhere, and do you know what he told me?

He didn't have any more ideas to help me. He said that
maybe I'd have to accept that I'd be depressed and anorexic
all my life! Well, I can't do that. It's so insane that it makes
me scream. . . . He even had the audacity to ask me for
suggestions to help me. Like I should really know! God, I
hate him, I hate him, and I've lost two more pounds and IT'S
ALL HIS FAULT! I need help, but I don't know where to
turn. The thought of trying to explain ALL OVER AGAIN
the fact that I have anorexia scares me. My parents and I
never talk about my eating disorder, and oh, God, I want to
die. The last person I could still count on just told me
there's nothing he could do! He was the third therapist I've
seen in three years. But you know, I want to overcome this
anorexia. I guess it's selfish, but I want to be able to tell
myself, "You did something." But that day may never come,
and I wonder if the fight would even be worthwhile. I'm so
hurt and humiliated. Please, I'm begging you, help me!

Sincerely,
Sydney B.

It's not hard to see that the trust base is eroded in Sydney's situation, that it's causing miscommunications between
the therapist and client. Sydney is dissatisfied with the amount
of therapy and seems frustrated that nothing's happening.
Their first major miscommunication: she didn't discuss this
when it first began to bother her (prior to her writing the first
letter to me). By the time she finally took the appropriate
action and explained how she felt (sometime between the first
and second letter), she convinced herself that the therapist
hated her. It's hard to trust someone you think hates you.
That led to their second major episode of miscommunication:
because she believed he hated her, she misinterpreted what
he said and didn't challenge it when she heard it. So when
the therapist admitted he was out of ideas, Sydney heard it
as, "I refuse to work with you (because you know I hate you),"

or worse, "I can't cure you." When she heard him say she had a choice to make: accept your situation or get the therapy moving in the right direction by taking some responsibility for your own recovery, she got angry at him, thought he was giving up, and felt abandoned. Instead of talking with him about this, she lost more weight and blamed him. What she needed to say to her therapist — but didn't — was what came across in her letter: she was scared of having to take responsibility for her own actions, she was scared of having to go it alone (her parents seemed to be out of the picture), she didn't trust herself to get over the anorexia by herself, and she needed a therapist to help her even if she seemed to fight him every step of the way. Sydney both needed and wanted someone to count on, someone to tell her what to do to get better.

So you see, the process of therapy can be frustrating without that base of trust. You need trust to get through the tough discussions with your therapist. You also need time. Therapy takes time and is a cooperative venture, like the relationship between a coach and an athlete. The therapist and coach do similar things — give you accurate information, teach you strategies for dealing with an opponent, and motivate you to develop skills and control.

But just as there are coaches with different styles of motivating their athletes, therapists, too, can have different styles. Although all therapists are catalysts for change, some are very directive and expect you to depend on them to give you the answers (Sydney seemed to want a therapist like that) while others give you a lot of responsibility for your own recovery and want you to rely more on yourself than on them to find the solutions to your problems (that's how Sydney's therapist seemed to be working with her). It's important to consider this issue of style when you look for a therapist, since therapy works best when there's a good fit and a comfortable chemistry between you and the person you've decided to let help you. An athlete and someone in therapy have similar jobs — to follow the suggestions of the person teaching them, and do the work by using their own skills and insights, which have been enhanced by the coach's or therapist's input. Therapy teaches you skills and provides a time framework within which you can safely and comfortably allow yourself to grow and change in productive ways.

There are different therapy formats. Sometimes it's one-on-one, as just described: that's called *individual therapy*. There are many kinds of individual therapies. Some are referred to as long-term, which means you can expect to be meeting with your therapist at least once a week for a year or more. One example of *long-term therapy* is *psychoanalysis*, which involves a lot of talking and focusing on your past as a way of understanding what's happening to you now. *Short-term therapy* is designed to last less than a year, often less than six months. Several types of therapies lend themselves to brief time frames. For instance, there's *behavioral therapy*, which teaches you how to change your behaviors but doesn't require that you do a lot of verbal self-analysis about why those behaviors came to play a part in your life. *Cognitive therapy* teaches you to recognize the unproductive ways in which you think and talk about yourself, understand how the old ways contributed to the development and maintenance of your eating disorder, and change the old ways so that the eating disorder can be challenged. *Cognitive-behavioral therapy* blends those two formats. A short-term format usually feels very structured, with its specific goals and limited time frame for achieving those goals explained to you at the outset.

Family members may also be involved in the discussions with you and the therapist (regardless of whether your format is long-term or short-term, in-patient or out-patient). This is called *family therapy*, and it can be very useful in supporting your efforts to overcome anorexia and/or bulimia because it helps you pinpoint areas of friction that you may not have realized contributed to the eating disorder. For instance, frustrated by the anorexia or bulimia, it's common for a parent to ask, "Why don't you just start eating like you used to?" — a question that not only gets you angry if you're the person with the eating disorder but signals that there's a lot of misunderstanding within the family about the nature of eating disorders. In any family, people get angry at one time or another, but in eating-disorder families, the anger doesn't get resolved quickly or easily and that's one reason why family therapy can be of use.

> When I was really into the bulimia I think the anger about it was the kind that alienated me from my family, that really put a wall between us. Now that I'm recovering, I've learned to express my anger and turn it into something that informs all of us. But we needed the family sessions to learn that and learn how to handle our anger.
>
> *Jeannie G., age seventeen*

A recent survey of families in which someone had an eating disorder asked all family members to rate their family environments. The results showed that difficulties with open expression of feelings (any feelings, not just angry ones), conflict, and lack of support between family members were pressing issues (Source: Stephen L. Stern et al., "Family Environment in Anorexia Nervosa and Bulimia," *International Journal of Eating Disorders*, 8, no. 1 [1989]: 25–31). Family therapy sessions can help all of you feel safer identifying and talking about such areas of friction and can help each of you understand that confronting and conquering an eating disorder doesn't have to be (and isn't) the sole responsibility of an anorectic or bulimic.

There's another major advantage to family therapy sessions: they give everyone the opportunity to discuss really difficult situations, such as having to acknowledge and cope with the alcoholism (or any addiction) of a family member, the mental illness of a family member, or having the courage to admit that you or someone else in your family has been a victim of psychological or physical abuse. The following letter expresses the range of emotions that can be generated when you have to face such issues,

Dear Nancy,

I don't often admit that I have a disorder. I was hospitalized for two months, and I am still following up in outpatient treatment once a week.

I had become dependent on Ex-Lax and I rarely ate over 600 calories a day. My mother noticed a change in my bathroom habits, which had become too difficult to hide. A lot of times I would have a bowel movement in my sleep. I was taking a daily dose of thirty Ex-Lax pills.

My father didn't really think I had a problem. He felt I was just doing it for attention so I should be watched constantly. The school nurse thought I needed professional help and suggested I see a doctor. I did, I gained, and was discharged, but now I'm back to my old ways in spite of the outpatient work. I am so afraid to bring up deep issues. I don't want to reexperience the pain and I don't want to have people see me crying about past issues. My father was abusive, mostly verbally but occasionally physically. I was always blamed for things my sisters and brothers did because I was the oldest.

I was on antidepressants but I quit taking them. I guess right now I'm not choosing life. I'm really struggling with that. I hope I will make the right decision, life. I have a lot of friends looking out for me who won't let me slip through their fingers, but I guess if I wanted to die that bad, I would.

I found your book was helpful in pointing out prevention measures, which I will use on my younger sisters. No one should have to punish themselves for love, respect, or acceptance.

Sincerely,
Charlotte H.

It isn't unusual for a person to develop an eating disorder as a response to familial alcoholism or abuse, and as hard as it is to admit you're anorectic or bulimic, it can be even harder to own up to the probability that something in the way your family operates has played a part in your eating problem. You tend to want to protect your family and often feel as if the responsibility for family harmony and happiness falls on your shoulders. But that isn't your sole responsibility — and family therapy can be a safe place in which you and your family address and resolve many of the delicate and sensitive issues that may be propelling your eating disorder. As Charlotte so poignantly said, "No one should have to punish themselves for love, respect, or acceptance."

Group therapy involves meeting with several unrelated people who have similar problems (such as eating disorders) and are seeing the same therapist you are. All of you get together with the therapist to explore the problems you have in common and, it is hoped, find solutions. You can participate in a group at the same time you are involved in individual and/or family therapy, but some therapists will have you join a group *when* you've finished with individual and/or family therapy but are still not quite ready to handle things totally on your own. In that case, the group becomes a source of information and support and can help you make the transition to life without one-on-one therapy.

Sometimes it's very scary to join a group.

It was the most humiliating thing in my life when I walked into the first group session and saw five people from my

school. I knew then that my secret was out and that I'd
really have to face up to my anorexia. I thought it'd be
blabbed all over school the next day: "Ann's in therapy.
Ann's got an eating disorder." As if everyone didn't already
know.

Ann B., age fifteen

Ann freaked out for the wrong reasons. Groups operate according to two principles that prevent humiliation and "blab-
bing." First, people who participate in therapy groups must
pledge to maintain confidentiality. That means nobody will
reveal what is said inside the group to anyone outside the
group unless specific permission is given to do so. Addition-
ally, people in groups must agree that any criticism directed
to a group member be constructive. If those conditions are
missing from a group in which you are a participant, find
another group.

Self-help is another form of therapy that is very useful
for people struggling with anorexia and bulimia. Eating-
disorder self-help groups are usually composed of anorectics
and bulimics in various stages of crisis or recovery, their families, and friends, along with trained professionals who sit in
on the groups in case of a crisis but do not necessarily assume
the role of leader or therapist. Self-help groups are sometimes
called support groups, because their purpose is to offer support to people whose lives have been touched and negatively
affected by eating disorders. Self-help is not a replacement
for professional therapy; it's an additional resource, sometimes
a very good one. Self-help is also inexpensive; groups are free
or charge a minimal membership fee, publish newsletters,
have monthly meetings with speakers, and several have hot-
lines for you to call when you're feeling really down. Self-help
groups are places to go to make new friends and to get back
your interpersonal skills, skills that anorexia and bulimia tend
to erase.

It might surprise you that many people with bulimia attend meetings of Overeaters Anonymous (O.A.), an organization founded in 1960 for compulsive overeaters and patterned after the twelve-step program of Alcoholics Anonymous (A.A.). For some bulimics the strict requirements of O.A. — that you limit yourself to three meals a day and nothing more, that you restrict your range of foods at meals, that you avoid sugars and other binge-triggering substances, that you check in with your sponsor by phone every day, and that you attend O.A. meetings weekly (and sometimes daily) — are comforting and helpful (Source: Roxanne Malenbaum et al., "Overeaters Anonymous: Impact on Bulimia," *International Journal of Eating Disorders*, 7, no. 1 [1988]: 139–43). For other bulimics the O.A. system seems to increase eating-disordered thoughts and behaviors, such as the inappropriate focus on foods and the desire to binge. How you respond to a self-help group is a very personal matter, and if you don't like a particular program, it doesn't mean you're wrong or that the program's bad — it just means you have to keep searching until you find the right fit for you.

There are still more options for people who are looking for help confronting and conquering their eating disorders. Sometimes, if you are under the care of a physician, your treatment may include the use of prescription medications. According to Dr. James Mitchell, *drug therapy* for eating disorders evolved from attempts to treat certain symptoms of anorexia and bulimia with drugs originally developed for other diagnoses (Source: "Psychopharmacology of Eating Disorders," in *The Psychobiology of Human Eating Disorders*, 41– 49. New York: The New York Academy of Sciences, 1989). For example, antidepressants, which work to ease the symptoms of depressed patients, are sometimes prescribed for bulimics, since bulimics often show signs of being depressed. If you have been given a prescription for any of the following: Nardil, Marplan, Parnate, Prozac, Elavil, Tofranil, or

Sinequan, you are taking a form of antidepressant medication. A medication with the chemical name of cyproheptadine hydrochloride (trade name: Periactin) originally used as an antihistamine for patients with allergies, has been found to stimulate appetites; it is now sometimes prescribed for anorectics.

Lately, there has been a lot of controversy about how useful drugs really are for helping people overcome their eating disorders. Some of the antidepressants in the chemical category of monoamine oxidase inhibitors (such as Nardil) require that you avoid certain meats, dairy products, and alcoholic beverages while taking them. Since the point of eating-disorder therapy is to get you *less* obsessed about your food intake and the medication requires that you be very diligent about that food intake, those two aspects of the therapy could sometimes work against each other. Another consideration is that taking antidepressant drugs can cause serious side effects, such as nausea, heart palpitations, skin rashes, bloating, constipation, dizziness, drowsiness, and blood pressure changes. (And that's just a partial list; side effects differ according to the chemical composition of your particular drug. Make sure to ask your doctor about this.)

These things all have an impact on the issue of compliance. Compliance means that you agree to do what your doctor tells you to do. You may have every intention of taking the medication but when it comes down to actually swallowing those pills each day, you don't! Sometimes it's because of the physical side effects just mentioned; sometimes it's because you discover you're opposed to "drugs," worry about getting hooked, and classify any kind of pill as something harmful. Sometimes the pill-taking issue becomes yet another topic to battle about with your parents, a power struggle of " 'they want me to do' versus 'I want to do.' " Sometimes you forget to take a pill at the designated time because you're too busy or you're embarrassed to have to go to the school nurse's office to get the medication. Some kids don't like to have to go to their doctors for the blood tests required to monitor the amounts of medication in their bodies, so they take themselves off the antidepressants against the advice of their physicians. The bottom line is that if you don't take the medication as it's prescribed, it won't have the chance to work to your advantage. If you have any concerns about something prescribed as a part of your therapy, it is your right and also your responsibility to ask questions and to find out what you can expect to happen if you do take the pills and what can happen if you don't.

Therapy for eating disorders should include consultations with a nutritionist, who will determine if your understanding of the role of food and nutrition in your life is accurate, will correct any misinformation, and can help you devise meal plans and eating strategies to combat your food-related obsessions and compulsions. Some anorectics and bulimics find that nutritionists are their most valuable resource and that therapy wouldn't work as well without them.

Why? Nutritionists are as keyed into food as you are, which provides an instantaneous bond between you. The difference is, however, that a nutritionist has the facts about food straight. It's hard to fool or con a nutritionist. If you try, you'll be confronted: accurate information will replace your inaccurate beliefs.

What might you learn? Here's a sampling of the kinds of information your nutritionist might share with you.

- 3,500 calories equal one pound of fat, and whether it's 3,500 calories' worth of chicken or 3,500 calories' worth of potato chips, the end result in terms of potential weight added to your body is the same (although your digestive system may respond differently to different foods).
- Older teenagers who've completed their growth (and adults) can safely lose weight on 1,200 to 1,400 calories

cathy®   by Cathy Guisewite

a day; to maintain an existing weight takes at least 1,800 calories a day for a normally active person. Any weight gain should be attempted slowly — much as a weight loss would be.

– A balanced diet for someone of your age, height, sex, and physical activity level includes foods from the following food groups: meat/poultry/seafood, fruits, vegetables (nonstarchy), breads/cereals/starches, milk and cheeses (including yogurts), fats and oils (such as butter, margarine, corn oil, nuts, seeds, peanut butter, avocados, etc.).

– Food exchanges make sticking to a meal plan easier. Many foods can be substituted for other foods with similar nutritional values, making it possible for you to build on your food preferences, gradually and safely normalizing your eating patterns. For instance, if you hate to drink milk but are supposed to drink skim or low-fat milk, you can substitute low-fat yogurt or any low-fat cheese such as mozzarella, ricotta, or cottage cheese. If you're supposed to drink whole milk, you could substitute something like cheddar cheese or whole-milk yogurt. If you're supposed to eat bread and don't enjoy it, you can have a taco or a tortilla; if you can't stand red meat, a serving of canned tuna or salmon would do, and so on.

– Muscle weighs more than fat. The number you see on your scale isn't necessarily an accurate reflection of how "fat" you are. (For more information regarding nutrition, see Appendix B.)

Therapy can take place in a number of settings. If you're physically ill when you begin therapy you may find yourself living in a hospital for a while as an in-patient in a special section called an "eating-disorder unit," where the doctors and nurses are trained to care for your unique needs and where the patients share similar problems. When therapy doesn't involve such hospitalization, you'd meet at the doctor's or therapist's office for a certain number of hours each week. Self-help groups frequently convene in rented space at local churches or hospitals, and sometimes even take place in members' homes. A word of caution, however. There are some unethical therapists in practice who may try to take advantage of your vulnerability and trust. *If a therapist suggests you get involved on a sexual level, get out of the situation immediately, tell your parents or guardian, and report that therapist to the local authorities.* What such a person is suggesting isn't therapy; it's sexual coercion. This is not to suggest that there are many therapists who would do such things — there aren't — but if even one did, it's enough to warrant this note of caution.

If you have anorexia and/or bulimia and agree to go into therapy, you may find yourself involved in all of these forms of therapy with several different health care professionals, depending on your needs and stage of recovery, and also depending on who's available in your community to help you. It sounds more complicated than it really is. You won't be faced all at once with everything just described. Therapy unfolds; it doesn't bowl you over. In any case, therapy isn't something to be afraid of. It's an opportunity to be challenged and show you can meet the challenge and come out ahead.

Thinking about Change

It can be overwhelming to think about confronting your eating disorder with the help of someone who'll start out as a stranger. Your expectations of getting anywhere may be very low, especially if you've tried to shake the anorexia or bulimia in the past and failed. In fact, your experience may have been like walking on a treadmill on which you took a step forward and then got pushed two steps back, so that you were constantly losing ground as you struggled to make progress. It's not unreasonable to feel skeptical and scared. Because any change puts some unknowns into your life, and you're about to look for someone to help you make some positive changes, try the Anticipation Exercise to help you clarify your fears and anxieties about altering your life-style from that of someone with an eating disorder to that of someone without one, and to help you cope with or avoid feelings of panic as you contemplate the possibility of change.

The Anticipation Exercise

Life is filled with stumbling blocks that get in the way of things you want to accomplish, that make goals a little harder to reach. Your present goal is to fight your eating disorder and win. You realize that there will be big battles along the way, some of which you may lose, but *you will emerge victorious.*

Your task is to describe the stumbling blocks as you anticipate them. For each stumbling block indicate what you will do to either neutralize it or get around it so that it will no longer be a problem for you. If you plan to have allies helping you, indicate who they are and what their roles will be. Keep a permanent record of what you've thought about. You can do it as a list, with columns headed *Stumbling Block, Removal Strategy, Allies,* or as a narrative or story. Make sure you come up with a concrete description you can refer back to.

Anticipation is one thing, but doing something to implement change is another. It will be a little easier to accomplish if you'll let yourself think about (and try to believe) the following facts:

- an eating disorder is like a tough adversary that needs a well-prepared, carefully coached opponent if it's going to be licked;
- the effort will be worth it;
- you deserve to be helped;

  – you're not a "bad" person if you've tried and failed before
    this;

  – a relapse of an eating disorder you thought you'd con-
    quered doesn't mean you've failed, or that your past
    efforts were for nothing, or that you're doomed to live
    with anorexia or bulimia forever. Try to think of a relapse
    as an opportunity to learn more about yourself and your
    situation, a reminder that you need to communicate
    clearly and be an assertive person.

Tell yourself over and over, "I'm worth it," even if you don't
really feel that way right now.

Your Role in Finding the Help You Need

You've made the decision that you need outside help and
want to find it. Locating the person (or combination of people)
to guide you out of the eating-disorder maze may seem even
more of a challenge to you than making the initial decision
was. But taking an active role in choosing a therapist can make
the difference between being successful in your effort to conquer the eating disorder or failing at it. It means you'll have
to do some more soul-searching.

Teenagers and young adults don't usually have much
experience in deciding who's going to be responsible for their
health care and don't usually know where and how to find
such people. They are probably more accustomed to having
their parents or guardians make these recommendations and
decisions. Think about how much input you've had in picking
a pediatrician or dentist or even a therapist if you've seen one
in the past. If you're like most young people, you've probably
had little or none.

Yet as you become more mature it's completely reasonable to want to have some input into these decisions. While finding such help — if you're under the age of twenty-one — is probably still going to be handled by your family, you should try to take an active role in the decision-making process. After all, it's your body and your mind that are being entrusted to another person's care, and the care-giving/care-accepting relationship should be based on mutually satisfactory expectations.

This is very important when you're anorectic and/or bulimic and you're trying to regain control of your eating behaviors. You *must* be able to trust the person who's going to help you in your quest and you must be willing to have that person confront you about issues in ways that may make you very uncomfortable, angry, even emotionally hurt. It's to your advantage to have that guide be a trained professional who has had experience working with anorectics and bulimics. As a reminder, in case you've forgotten, any of the following individuals or combination of these people — a medical doctor, psychologist, social worker, nutritionist, or a team of these professionals who work together, or someone from a self-help network who's been anorectic and/or bulimic, has struggled with the same issues you are, has conquered the problem, and is in a position to offer you help and hope from the perspective of someone who's "been there" — could be your choice.

That's not to say that family or close friends won't be helpful; they can be. But when your eating disorder is at an advanced stage you need someone who isn't emotionally involved with you to be your *primary* resource. You need someone who can be objective and see things from the perspective of an outside observer. You've heard it said that a doctor should never treat his or her own family. That's because judgment is clouded by emotions. The same applies to your situation. The judgment and advice of family members or friends will be tempered by their intense feelings for you and attachment to you, and they probably won't be able to say what needs to be said.

Since the odds are that you have some preferences for the kind of person you'd like to spend such intense moments with, or the environment in which you'd be willing to embark on such therapy, it's very useful to think about these preferences and discuss them with your parents or guardian before deciding who will be your doctor or therapist.

However, having your preferences taken seriously by the adults who'll be paying for your health care means you'll have to be able to explain why these preferences are important to you. If you've thought things through ahead of time, you can then use the information as a basis from which to work together to locate a qualified doctor, therapist, therapy group, or self-help network, or at least reach a compromise between your preferences and your family's perceptions of your needs.

There's one exception to this negotiation process, however. *If your eating disorder has created a situation in which your life is currently in danger, your preferences won't be a factor in the immediate decisions your parents or guardians will have to make to save your life.* You may find yourself in an emergency room at a hospital, or in an eating-disorder unit, or on a psychiatric floor of a hospital. Until your health has stabilized to a point where life or death is not the overwhelming concern, don't expect to negotiate about your ideal therapy situation.

The following questions should help you start thinking about your preferences. Answer them honestly and write your responses on a sheet of paper.

1. Does the sex of the doctor or therapist you'll be seeing matter to you? If so, do you prefer a male or a female? What are your reasons for this preference?

For instance, if you're a girl, would you prefer to see a female doctor or therapist? If you're a boy, would you prefer going to a male doctor or therapist? Have you had either a particularly good or bad experience with a same-sex or opposite-sex doctor or therapist in the past that has caused you to feel this way?

2. Would you be willing to be seen by a doctor or therapist one of your friends or relatives had seen and recommended, or would you prefer going to someone no one else you know had been to? What are your reasons for your choice?

Some people find that knowing about a therapist's personality and reputation from the firsthand experience of a friend or relative eases the tension of initial visits and makes the thought of therapy a little less unnerving. On the other hand, you might be the kind of person for whom privacy and confidentiality is a major concern and the thought of anyone else knowing your therapist threatens you. Perhaps you might be concerned that if anyone even knew you were involved in a doctor-patient or therapist-client relationship, it might make it harder for you to speak openly and honestly.

3. Would the age of the doctor or therapist affect your initial reaction to him or her? Would it alter your willingness to work with the person? What are your reasons for thinking this?

For instance, could you discuss problems more openly with a younger therapist because you'd feel more in synch, or would you have more confidence in someone older who had more professional experience? Are you basing your

reasoning on actual past experiences with older vs. younger
teachers and doctors, or is your reasoning more a "guessti-
mate" based on gut feelings?

**4. Is there any chance that the location of the doctor's or
therapist's office might affect your willingness to work with
him or her?**

As odd a question as this may seem to be, many people
are put off by the location of some doctors' and therapists'
offices. This is often an issue at first when the location is within
a hospital complex, since some of us are afraid of hospitals
and don't even feel at ease walking in and out of one. Also,
a possible stumbling block to therapy is a location that's in-
convenient for you because it's hard to get to. Lots of people
get sloppy about keeping appointments if getting somewhere
is a big effort and when the payoffs from the therapy don't
seem to outweigh the inconvenience and time involved in
getting to therapy. Discuss this now so that office location
won't become an excuse for you to stop therapy after you have
begun it.

After you've written out your answers to these questions,
write down any other preferences and concerns about therapy
situations and have a complete list of *all* these questions,
preferences, and concerns prepared and in your hands when
you and your family are discussing who'll be hired to be your
therapist. If possible, have a duplicate copy for your family
to refer to during your conversations, and save the list and
your own copy so that later on you can share these questions
and concerns with your doctor, therapist, or self-help group.
Having your thoughts on paper is like being on stage with a
TelePrompTer to help you out when you're nervous and forget
your lines. You may flub what you say, but at least you'll be

able to make a quick recovery and keep the dialogue going in the direction you want it to.

During this selection process, keep the following in mind: if you don't hit it off with a therapist, you have the right to switch, but recognize that since you're dealing with a stranger about something with a lot of tension, it's natural to have awkward moments and it can take weeks or months for trust and comfort to develop. In addition, therapy requires effort on your part as well as on your therapist's part, and you have to be honest with your therapist to expect good results (see Appendix C).

Changing the Focus

Whatever decision you make, be sure to give yourself credit for answering questions and asking others. By approaching a problem logically and seeing it through to a satisfactory solution, you've exerted some control during the selection process and won't have to feel "done to" — even if the therapist or doctor isn't your ideal and you've had to make some compromises about what you'd hoped that person would be like. You've improved your odds of locating someone who'll prove to be your kind of counselor, not someone you'll resent seeing or who you'll be afraid to work with.

Finding help in this way — even if you know that the ultimate choice is really your family's and not yours — achieves one other important goal for you. It puts you in a different, healthy focus. It shows you're not willing to be placed in the "sick role" in the family anymore: you're not going to be passive for the rest of your life, you're not going to be afraid to stand up for yourself and be assertive. It actually forces other people to take notice that even if you're still struggling with an eating disorder you can be capable, rational, and in control of some components of your life. This is a way to build a foundation of competence — success breeds success, and confidence comes with competence.

To get to this point in your relationship with your family and friends, to be able to confront yourself and your eating disorder and admit the need for help and take the steps to find it, shows strength, growth, and guts. Even if you're in therapy as you read this chapter and are making strides toward health, you may experience from time to time that "one step forward, two steps back" sensation discussed earlier. If you do, to prevent the steps back from getting longer than the strides forward, try developing a personal Inside-out Plan. You're more ready now to do it than you've been before, and it's an exercise to help you acknowledge your strengths, take pride in them, and rely on them when times are tough.

The Inside-out Plan

People judge you by looking at externals. Friends and acquaintances pay attention to what you look like, the number of social groups you're part of, how many awards you win, the scores on your tests, how much money you have or earn, how many outfits you wear, and so on. Parents pay a lot of attention to how obedient you are, how you dress and wear your hair, how you do in school, and so on. It may seem as if nobody has the time or energy to listen to and know the *real* you. That can feel awful and often contributes to the power an eating disorder is able to exert over you. But you're going to make it possible for them to know the real you by looking inside yourself and getting out what's inside you (and, what counts more, who you really are, what you believe in, your potential).

The Inside-out Plan is a two-step process.

STEP #1: *"I am what I am."*

This step may take you a while to complete; don't worry about that. Its purpose is to teach you about yourself and to get you to the point where you can say "I am what I am" and feel comfortable and happy admitting that. You'll need to do the following:

– develop an intellectual understanding about eating disorders, why they happen, what can be done about them, and why you were vulnerable to them.

Obviously, you've begun this process by reading *When Food's a Foe*. Other books and magazine articles will be useful (see Suggested Readings). Being in therapy and asking lots of questions is another way of achieving this.

– make some mental pictures of yourself as you've been in the past and as you wish to be now.

Self-imagery is a great technique to use to get to know yourself well. Close your eyes and think about yourself. What do you see? What do you look like? What situations are you in? Who's with you? What's going on? How are you feeling? Do this several times, and make sure to include images of yourself as someone who is free of anorexia or bulimia. Take notes on each mental movie so you can describe it in detail after it's over and think about the things you saw.

Picturing yourself in positive situations makes it easier to turn those images into realities when you actually try to! In fact, a study at Harvard University done by Dr. Stephen Kosslyn and Carol Seger found that "people . . . reported using images to change their feelings, particularly to get in or out of a particular mood, or to motivate themselves" (*New York Times*, August 12, 1986, C6).

– discover and describe your gut feelings about everything from *a* to *z!*

This means giving yourself permission to feel things that you might not want to admit feeling, and to then put these feelings into words. It also means acknowledging good feelings and the situations and people that triggered them. You can do this in several ways, either by keeping a formal diary, taking abbreviated notes, or — if you have a small cassette tape recorder — by dictating into the machine as the feelings surface. Obviously, you won't be able to do a dictation in the middle of a class or at work, but you certainly could while at home.

STEP #2: *Share your discoveries with others you care about and if there are things you want to change, work together to bring about that change.*

The ball is in your court. You have a factual base from which to describe your situation, you've turned yourself inside out by exploring and acknowledging your gut feelings and setting them down in print or on tape, and you can say, "I am what I am," because you know yourself so well. The clarity with which you see yourself will make it easier to project that self-image and share it with others. It shouldn't matter so much to you if that image is a little tarnished. By now you should realize that no one's perfect and no one expects you to be, either.

A few words of advice, however: it's not necessary to reveal everything about yourself at once. If you're in therapy and people ask for details about it, such as "What did you talk about today?" or "What did the therapist have to say?" you may find that you don't want to answer those questions directly. Therapy can be emotionally and even physically draining, and you often need time and distance from the therapy session to digest what happened and to put to use the insights you've uncovered and the skills you've learned. So it's OK to politely and firmly decline to answer such questions or to say that you'll discuss this later on in the day or week. On the other hand, you might be so enthusiastic about what occurred during a particular therapy session that you want to shout it to the world, but nobody seems to want to listen to you! In that case, make some phone calls to friends, relatives, anyone who will hear you out! The point is, you decide who you want to share insights with, how much of yourself you want to reveal, and when it feels comfortable for you to do so.

Ask yourself a final question. It's a biggie. "Do you want things to change and stay changed?" You must be honest. As part of the answer, you need to think about where your family and friends fit into the picture both at present and in the future. It's just possible that you may need to change your social group, get out of some of the old relationships. It's also possible that you may need to get away from home for a while and live with other relatives or close friends to maintain the gains you've made in your mental health since confronting your eating disorder in therapy. Getting cured doesn't guarantee a fairy-tale ending.

But the bottom line is that you're worth it. Earlier in this chapter you were asked to say that to yourself over and over again, even if you didn't really believe it. Now it's time to write down all the reasons you are, in fact, worth going to all the trouble of getting your life back in balance. Write down at least ten reasons, but go for one hundred.

> It had been so long since I liked myself. That was the best part of going into therapy for the anorexia and bulimia — I found that what I had to say counted, and that made it possible for me to feel things. I didn't have to bury everything in my binges and I didn't have to hide from myself or anyone else anymore.
>
> *Henriette L., age eighteen*

8
HELPING SOMEONE WHO HAS AN EATING DISORDER

Wanting to help someone you care about work through a problem is a natural and praiseworthy impulse. Knowing how to help and understanding the limits of your effectiveness are more than an impulse; they are a skill. When the person you want to help is a victim of anorexia nervosa or bulimia, part of the skill includes understanding that your help may not be appreciated if the disorder has a very strong hold, and realizing that in spite of all your best efforts and good intentions there may be times when trying to help just doesn't pay.

Deciding What You Expect to Accomplish by Helping

My best friend, Arden, began dieting in ninth grade. By the beginning of tenth grade it was obvious she was an anorectic. She looked so skinny a lot of our classmates said that she grossed them out. They were turned off by her and turned their backs on her. She didn't seem to care, but I did. I tried to run interference for her. I defended her. I begged her to eat. I took her for a makeover, hoping the cosmetics person would tell her she looked lousy. The thanks I got was that last week she told me to get off her case, to stop lecturing her, and to mind my own business. She said we couldn't be friends anymore. I guess I was an idiot to want to help. She's killing herself. I wanted to stop her but I can't.

Allyn P., age sixteen

Allyn's experience is more common than uncommon. She reached out to a friend whose self-destructive path was obvious and got shot down in the process. She ended up feeling hurt and useless and had to face the fact that she was ineffective as a helper. Ineffective, that is, insofar as her goals were unrealistic. She was working toward a cure for Arden's problem, but she didn't have the skills nor was she in the right kind of relationship to bring about a cure. As a friend she did her best, but when you're dealing with eating disorders, friendship isn't always enough. Was there anything she could have done to change the outcome?

To start, Allyn would have been better off approaching the problem from an intellectual rather than an emotional point of view. She really needed to take some time to analyze the situation and come up with a personal definition of "helping." That way she would've had clear goals to aim for and if she didn't seem to be reaching them, *she* could have asked for help, changed her tactics, or abandoned the project altogether.

If this sounds unnecessarily clinical or harsh, it's only to point out that people with eating disorders develop abnormal habits and rituals that can interfere with interpersonal relationships. Since one of the side effects of anorexia and bulimia is to change the way its victims relate to other people in their lives, your good intentions may be misread. Caring may come across as coercion. Attempts at discussion may be construed as accusation. Your honesty may be heard as distortion of facts due to your jealousy. You run the risk of putting yourself in the position of a would-be rescuer (see Chapter 6), whose attempts at helping are likely to be met with angry, hostile reactions rather than open, friendly, appreciative ones. In short, you may get yourself into a no-win situation that ends up making you feel abused and hurt.

Helping an anorectic or bulimic necessitates getting involved, and that requires an interpersonal relationship. You really need to know what you might be in for, so if the worst happens and you fail, you won't be crushed by the experience. Before letting your helping impulse get you personally involved with someone who has an eating disorder (as opposed to being that person's therapist or self-help group leader), answer two tough questions: "What is it that I'm trying to accomplish by helping?" and "What's in it for me?" If you have no ulterior motives other than to be a friend (even if you're a relative) who's available to talk anytime, a resource for whoever's in trouble, that's fine. You may not expect anything in return beyond seeing that individual get well and feeling good about making a positive contribution to another human being's life. Even if your goal is to set an example and show the person you have problems too and it's possible to deal with them in less destructive ways than the eating-disorder route, that's OK because you're acting as a role model without forcing the issue.

Be honest, though. Are you expending such effort just as a gesture of your concern and affection for the other person, or are you trying to score points with the family or your mutual social circle for your competence and energy? If you're trying to teach the other person a lesson about eating disorders, if you're constantly challenging his or her obsessions and compulsions by being super rational and logical, you may not accomplish your goal and your help may be a turnoff. If you expect to impose a cure, and that's your major motivation for getting involved, forget it. If you're looking to exert some sort of control over the other person by helping, if you're very frightened by the eating disorder and by becoming involved you think you'll alleviate some of your own discomfort, it's probably best to back off and maintain a less intense relationship. You probably have some issues of your own to work on before trying to help someone in worse shape than you.

Five Rules to Make You a More Effective Helper

One of the best things you can do to make yourself an effective and appreciated helper is to develop a base of knowledge from which you operate. Again, don't worry if this makes you feel as if you need a Ph.D. in "helping" even to try to do what you think should be a natural act. It's a way to maximize your impact, a little like bodybuilding in the winter months so that when the warm weather comes along you won't end up like the ninety-eight-pound weakling who gets sand kicked in his face by the bullies. Eating disorders turn their victims into bullies, and tough ones at that. You can succeed if you keep a few simple rules in mind.

RULE #1: *Be informed.*

Learn all you can about anorexia and bulimia before offering help of any kind. By reading this book you will have an accurate knowledge base and will develop a sense of how complicated the problems are. This will allow you to make on-target judgments about the person you're trying to help, even if it's just to figure out (a) how serious the problem has become, and (b) what arguments the other person will use to try to prove you wrong.

RULE #2: *Make sure there really is a problem. If you know there's a problem, make sure the problem is the one you think it is!*

As obvious as this sounds, it's a rule that is easily forgotten.

I noticed scars on my girlfriend's knuckles soon after we'd started dating, and I knew she'd been going to the dentist a lot lately so I made the assumption that she was a bulimic with a really bad case of it. That's when I found out a little knowledge could be a dangerous thing. Instead of asking her point-blank, I kept sneaking in references to bingeing and how bad it was for you. I even looked through her bathroom cabinets for laxatives. I thought I could help her since she liked me so much and we got on so great. But she caught me snooping. She let me have it. Her scars were from an old riding accident and she was going to the dentist to have a crown on a molar repaired. We'll never go out again, she was that mad at me.

Randolph M., age seventeen

We can make a lot of assumptions about the things we *think* we see developing, as Randolph M. describes doing, and offer help based on two premises: that our assessment of the situation is correct (Randolph's wasn't) and that our solutions are workable, constructive, and accurate. All too often, they're not.

RULE #3: *Define the nature of your relationship with the person you want to help.*

To do so, answer the following questions.

1. What's your relationship to the person? (For example, parent, sibling, relative, friend, teacher, boyfriend, girlfriend, employer?)
2. How long have you known the person?
3. How well do you know the person?
4. Where do you know the person from? (For example, home, school, work, church or synagogue?)
5. Do you have a relatively formal relationship with that person, or do you relate more as equals? (Are you an

authority figure like a parent, teacher, or employer, who is more apt to be perceived as an "expert" rather than an equal? Is the relationship one in which there's no indication that one of you has higher standing than the other, even if you're an adult rather than a same-age friend, relative, or colleague?)

6. What's your style of communication with that person under normal, everyday circumstances? (Do you tend to lecture rather than discuss? Are you confidants who share innermost feelings and secrets, or do you speak openly but not exactly as confidant? Do you tend to speak your mind, or do you tend to leave a lot unsaid?)

The nature of your relationship will obviously be an influence on how your efforts will be interpreted. If you're a parent and the person with anorexia or bulimia is your child, and a teenager as well, the ordinary stress, strain, and intensity of an adolescent-adult relationship will color and magnify your child's reactions to your help. Even if you're 100 percent right, you might meet with more resistance than a nonrelative would. If you're in a formal relationship with the person you want to help, your attempts can be experienced as coercive or bullying. If you're confidants, you're liable to risk ruining that close relationship if the person isn't ready for help. If you're a casual acquaintance, you could come across as pushy or nosy. And if you're involved in a romantic/sexual relationship, tact, delicacy, and a heightened degree of understanding on your part are crucial if your helping efforts will be perceived as helpful. Here's why.

Ideally, a romantic/sexual relationship is an intense, emotional connection between two people who are also physically attracted to each other and who discover, over time, that they can trust each other. That trust makes it possible for them to share their innermost thoughts without fear of ridicule or exposure, and that trust allows the physical aspects of their attraction to blossom and find expression in a romantic context.

You may hear kids say, "Sex is the most natural thing in the world," and it may be, but physical/sexual expression can be an excruciatingly difficult issue for people with eating disorders. Since body-image issues are exaggerated in people with anorexia and bulimia, physical intimacy can be very difficult to achieve and maintain. Many young women who have eating disorders will say they feel fat and ugly even when they're slender and attractive. They tend to perceive themselves as body parts, scrutinizing their breasts, stomachs, hips, thighs, and buttocks instead of being able to look in the mirror and see themselves as whole people. Often, trust is replaced with doubt as they misinterpret other people's silly comments and jokes as insults and scorn.

> My fiancé came into my mom's living room when I was stretched out on her couch on my stomach. I guess my butt was up in the air, and Howie gave me a pat on it when he tried to sit down. I was horrified. I felt like all my fat must have been visible through my spandex. So then when he called me his "little whale," I freaked. I haven't even been able to let him see me in a bathing suit since that day! And he just doesn't understand.
>
> *Flo G., age twenty*

The special bonds between people who've been romantically linked are often changed when an eating disorder comes into play. So if you're trying to help a girlfriend, you can't assume that she'll respond to you as she did before the eating disorder became an issue and/or was acknowledged. You must remind yourself that because she's insecure about her physical self, she's likely to be insecure about how you view her, and she may automatically assume you see her as the imperfect person she feels herself to be. An eating disorder often changes and even replaces communication — once her situation is revealed, your girlfriend may seem guarded, shying away from discussing and sharing the confidences that used to be so much a part of what made you a couple.

So what do you do? Ask her if she's ready to hear your perceptions about how the eating disorder has altered things between the two of you. If she says yes, tell her how you feel. If it hurts you to see her do this to herself, explain why. If she's willing to have you help her and that makes you happy, let her know. If you don't understand what she's doing, ask questions. But reassure her that your purpose in asking questions isn't to blame her but to educate yourself so that you can really be there for her, support her, and help her. Explain that if you get frustrated with her, it doesn't mean you think she's a bad person — it just means you're frustrated!

Give her permission to tell you to back off if you're moving too fast for her or if she feels you're prying or pressuring. Talk about how she wants to handle socially oriented eating situations such as going out to dinner with you and other friends. Does she want you to signal her if she looks like she's about to panic or if she seems to be bingeing in a restaurant? Does she want you to watch what she's eating or does she want you to ignore her food-related behaviors?

If there are intimacy issues that you want to discuss, ease into the topic, respect her heightened insecurity about her own physical self, and don't bombard her with a list of grievances. If you love her, say it again and again. If you find her attractive, tell her everything about her that attracts you and don't let her dwell on "fat issues." If she seems to withdraw from physical intimacy, respect her need for distance and ask her what you can do to help her begin to feel more comfortable within her physical self again. If you're willing to let the relationship continue during her recovery, try to think positively and talk positively. You might want to discuss some of the following possibilities: how the physical/intimate aspects of your relationship could become enhanced as a result of your increased sensitivities to each other's needs and wants, how the emotional commitments you've made to each other could be strengthened because you've chosen to stick with the relationship in spite of the stress of an eating disorder, and how it feels to ask for and receive unconditional support from another person.

There's always the possibility that no matter what your relationship, your efforts *may* be met with great relief and appreciation on the part of the other person, relief because someone has finally forced the issue at the right time and made the notion of self-control or cure a possibility.

RULE #4: *A person with an eating disorder must want to be helped and/or be ready to accept help for your efforts to have a positive impact on the situation.*

Unfortunately, unless that person comes to you for help or confides in you before you give in to your urge to help, you may not know about this state of readiness so you may or may not be an effective helper. This is why the next rule is so important.

RULE #5: *Make sure that you understand — both intellectually and emotionally — that there will be times when your help is effective, but, in spite of all your good intentions, there will also be times when you can't help someone who is struggling with an eating disorder.*

It may be as simple a matter as being at the right place at the right time, or as complicated as having a well-thought-out plan for therapy. So this is a rule even people in the helping professions — doctors, therapists, counselors, psychologists — must learn. They can't impose a cure simply by virtue of their knowledge and expertise, and there are no guarantees that what works for one client will work for all. If you are trying to help anorectics and bulimics, you must be ready to fail and not to give up if you do.

The Importance of the Time Frame

What makes one person ready to be helped and another resistant to help is in part a function of how long the eating disorder has been in place. Remember that anorexia and bulimia are abnormal behaviors that take on the characteristics of obsessions, compulsions, even addictions, and gain more and more control of their victims the longer they're allowed to persist. So you must understand that if the person you're trying to help has dieted down to eighty pounds and is 5'8" and insists on losing more weight to get rid of an imagined bulging stomach and cellulite-filled thighs, or if the person can't eat a meal without vomiting immediately afterward and won't go for more than a day without a binge of two hours' duration, you're not confronting someone who can hear your words of caution, logic, or concern. You're trying to work with someone who's the equivalent of a critically ill patient. Unless you're a therapist you probably won't be of much help at that point, though your concern may be appreciated by family members and you'll feel good about yourself for trying. But if you're trying to help someone whose anorexia and bulimia aren't so firmly entrenched in that person's behavior patterns, you stand a better chance of succeeding as long as you have the knowledge base, understand the rules just discussed, and have reasonable motivations urging you on.

When Total Honesty Isn't Always the Best Policy

A person with an eating disorder usually has a lot of self-doubt, and often comes from a background in which communication skills are lacking or absent. That's why so many anorectics and bulimics don't feel comfortable, may not feel they have the right, and may not even know how to speak up for themselves and clearly state what their needs and expectations are. Over a long period of time such unexpressed thoughts and emotions build to a pressure point that's uncomfortable and needs an outlet. The eating disorder develops and becomes the outlet for their pent-up feelings.

When you're determined to help such an individual, it's

Bloom County   by **Berke Breathed**

not always the best policy to be brutally honest and call things as you see them.

 – You could accidently threaten that person's already un-steady sense of self and make things worse rather than better by creating another layer of anxiety and increasing the person's need to turn to the eating disorder for safety.
 – You may overstep the bounds of decorum as that person defines it, because to an individual who hasn't developed the habit of speaking out and speaking up, someone who does so may be perceived as pushy, nosy, brazen, or worse — a raving lunatic who doesn't deserve to be lis-tened to.

How can you be honest without being perceived as a threat or possibly harming the person by your efforts? Don't be the person's judge and jury. Don't come off as an accuser. Do use "I language." For example, saying, "I love you and I'm worried about what your eating habits are doing to your health because I really care about you" is "I language." But saying, "Your eating habits are killing you, and if you knew how much I cared you'd understand why I'm mentioning this" doesn't give the same emotional message, even though it's meant to convey the same factual information. The person hears the accusing "your eating habits are killing you" and not only is it scary because it's probably true, but it obliterates the caring message hidden in the rest of the sentence.

There are other things you shouldn't tell eating-disorder victims, even if you really think them. *Don't ever say* — even in jest — "I wish I could have anorexia for a week or two," or "I know just what you're going through because I have weight concerns, too." You don't know what they're going through unless you've been there yourself, and being con-cerned with your weight or your body-image isn't the same as having an eating disorder. People who joke about being anorectic really mean to say they wish their bodies could be thinner. If that's what you want to discuss, say it that way instead. Don't make anorexia seem like a desirable state, especially to someone who might grasp at any straw to justify continuing that behavior.

Use the Golden Rule in deciding what you can discuss and how honest you can be. Try to imagine yourself at a stressful period in your life. Think about the kinds of people who you'd want to turn to for help or who you'd be willing to listen to. Think about the things that might be better left unsaid. Very few of us can handle complete self-disclosure even if we're not coping with a major problem in our lives. That's true for anorectics and bulimics too. Leave the confrontation for therapists, who have the skills to do it.

When Your Help Is Rejected but You Still Want to Help

There are few things that feel as bad as being rejected by another person. No matter how prepared you are for that possibility when you're interacting with a person with an eating disorder, it hurts. Rejection isn't necessarily the result of your doing something wrong. It may be a signal that the eating disorder has too strong a hold and professional intervention is necessary. Sometimes it may mark a transition phase in the person's eating disorder, from the less serious to more severe stages in which a mental barrier develops that makes it hard for the anorectic or bulimic to be a "people person," and which excludes almost everything else in his or her life that used to be significant. And that includes you.

Sometimes the rejection stems from your putting too much pressure on the person, and you're told where to go. Sometimes the reasons aren't clear but the message is. Your phone calls will be refused. If you stop by to visit, no one will

answer the door or you'll be told the person is out or un-
available. You might even get the silent treatment if you try
to talk face-to-face.

Let's assume that you believe the rejection has come
about because the eating disorder has colored and changed
the individual's perception of you and isn't an indication that
you've blown everything or that the state of your relationship
is irreversibly damaged. In other words, you feel that if the
eating disorder could be brought under control you could
resume your relationship in its pre-disorder state. So you want
to keep helping in some way, to prove your commitment to
the person. What can you do?

One suggestion is to write letters. If all your other attempts at communication are rejected, at least the mail will
get delivered. Of course, the mail may get pitched unread,
but it's more likely that someone will save your letters till the
other person's ready to read them.

Another possibility is to keep a diary of the little events
that used to involve both of you. Talk about what it feels like
not to have the other person's company and input. If the
person has had to drop out of school or work, and there's a
way of expanding the diary into a scrapbook with clips from
school newspapers or work memos or newspapers, photos of
friends and colleagues, even silly little things like notes passed
in class (or social notices from work), do so with the idea that
in a month or two — or whenever the time seems right —
you'll present it to the person to show that a thread exists
between you even if there's both a physical as well as a psychological separation. If you have access to a video camera,
you can create a similar record of the life you used to share
with this person by taping the little (and big) things that go
on at school, with friends, etc. You can make an even more
personal and private tape that just reveals your thoughts and
reactions: at home, set the video camera on a tripod and record
yourself talking directly to your friend. Don't turn off the tape

if you find yourself getting choked up or even crying — watching you being vulnerable and open can make it easier for your friend to risk that kind of emotional connection with you later on, when she's ready.

Understand that it's also OK to want to give up. There's only so much one person can do for another person, and we all have our inborn limits to our tolerance levels, patience levels, and pain levels. Knowing when you've reached your breaking point and stopping whatever it is that has brought you to the brink is just as important to your own health and well-being as is the gesture of helping someone else regain or retain theirs.

Is There Life after Rejection?

There is life after rejection, and frequently it includes the people who rejected you. Sometimes it happens because of your efforts to maintain contact while estranged. When the person with the eating disorder starts to get control of the disorder, communication may get reinstated because the person's "world view" is now able to readmit those other people who used to be significant.

Sometimes the impetus comes from the person even if you've given up your helping efforts. Usually, this occurs after the person's had some professional therapy and wants to pick up the pieces of his or her life and start fresh. The expectation is that since the relationship existed before, it has a chance to exist again.

Do you take this individual back with open arms? Do you say, "I forgive you for all the garbage you heaped on me"? Do you say, "I'll give you another chance, but just one. No more Mr. Nice Guy!"? It all depends. Now you're in the driver's seat and you have to decide the direction in which you want to go.

Your overwhelming need may be to clear the air and

relate the experience from your point of view, and maybe even lay a little guilt trip of your own. There's no place for guilt in this situation, because it won't change the past and may hurt the future status of your relationship. Clearing the air is another thing, depending on the stage of recovery the anorectic or bulimic is in. If it's someone just out of a hospital situation, connecting with you is a triumph in itself and it's unreasonable to expect to be able to clear the air. If it's someone who has been recovered for a period of months, seems to have his or her life in order, and is even involved in a self-help group and is counseling others, then it would be more reasonable to suggest sitting down and doing a postmortem. Here, too, apply the Golden Rule and treat the other person with respect.

No matter what happens, remember that you're only human and the other person is only human, too. Whatever else may result from trying to help someone get through a tough time, you will learn a lot about yourself, about your inner resources, and what it feels like to really give your all for someone else. Even if their outcome is less than perfect, your outcome is that you've shown the good stuff you're made of.

SUGGESTED READINGS

Abraham, Suzanne and Llewellyn-Jones, Derek. *Eating Disorders: The Facts.* Oxford: Oxford University Press, 1984.

Arbetter, Sandra R. "Eating Disorders: Emotional Food Fights." *Current Health 2,* 15 (March 1989): 1.

Atrens, Dale M. *Don't Diet.* New York: William Morrow, 1988.

Bennett, William and Gurin, Joel. *The Dieter's Dilemma: Eating Less and Weighing More.* New York: Basic Books, 1982.

Boston Children's Hospital, Baker, Susan, and Henry, Roberta R. *Parents' Guide to Nutrition: Healthy Eating from Birth Through Adolescence.* Reading, Mass.: Addison-Wesley, 1986.

Brody, Jane. "For Men and Boys, Anorexia and Bulimia (Often Undetected) Pose Special Problems." *New York Times,* August 16, 1990: B7, B13.

Bruch, Hilde. *The Golden Cage: The Enigma of Anorexia Nervosa.* Cambridge, Mass.: Harvard University Press, 1978.

_____. *Conversations With Anorexics.* New York: Basic Books, 1988.

Chernin, Kim. *The Obsession: Reflections on the Tyranny of Slenderness.* New York: Harper & Row, 1981.

_____. *The Hungry Self: Women, Eating, and Identity.* New York: Times Books, 1985.

Gilchrist, Ellen. "The Last Diet." In *Drunk with Love,* 146–58. Boston: Little, Brown, 1986.

Karlsberg, Elizabeth. "The Big Fat Lie: When Thin Does You In." *Teen,* 33 (July 1989): 29.

Lawrence, Marilyn, ed. *Fed Up and Hungry: Women, Oppression and Food.* New York: Bedrict, 1987.

Levenkron, Steve. *Kessa.* New York: Basic Books, 1986.

Newman, Jennifer. "Dieting: Beyond Good and Evil." *American Health,* 9 (September 1990): 90.

O'Neill, Cherry Boone. *Starving for Attention*. New York: Continuum, 1982.

Orbach, Susie. *Hunger Strike: The Anorectic's Struggle as a Metaphor for Our Age*. New York: W. W. Norton and Co., 1986.

Rosenfield, Anne R. "New Treatment for Bulimia." *Psychology Today*, 23 (March 1989): 28.

Roth, Geneen. *Feeding the Hungry Heart: The Experience of Compulsive Eating*. New York: NAL Books, 1982.

_____. *When Food Is Love: Exploring the Relationship Between Eating and Intimacy*. New York: Dutton, 1991.

Rusting, Ricki. "Starvaholics? Anorexics May Be Addicted to a Starvation 'High,'" *Scientific American*, 259 (November 1988): 35.

Sandmaier, Marian. "Eating Binges Can Be Contagious." *Mademoiselle*, 95 (March 1989): 146.

Schotte, David E. and Stunkard, Albert J. "Bulimia vs. Bulimic Behaviors on a College Campus." *JAMA*, 258 (September 1, 1987): 1213.

Siegel, Michele et al. *Surviving an Eating Disorder: New Perspectives and Strategies for Family and Friends*. New York: Harper & Row, 1988.

Werner-Berley, Judith. "Perfect Bodies to Die For." *McCall's*, 117 (May 1990): 61.

Wolf, Naomi. *The Beauty Myth: How Images of Beauty Are Used Against Women*. New York: William Morrow, 1991.

The following books and the journal are written for the people who will be your therapists. They are technical and based on the assumption that their readers have backgrounds in psychology and some medical knowledge. You might want to ask the people you've chosen to lead you out of the eating-disorder maze (1) if they have these books (or have access to them) and (2) if they would make them available to you and your family should you want to look through them.

Blinder, Barton J. et al. *The Eating Disorders: Medical and Psychological Bases of Diagnosis and Treatment.* New York: PMA Publishing Corp., 1988.

Brownell, Kelly D. and Foreyt, John P., eds. *Handbook of Eating Disorders: Physiology, Psychology, and Treatment of Obesity, Anorexia, and Bulimia.* New York: Basic Books, 1986.

Cash, Thomas F. and Pruzinsky, Thomas, eds. *Body Images: Development, Deviance, and Change.* New York: The Guilford Press, 1990.

Emmett, Steven W., ed. *Theory and Treatment of Anorexia Nervosa and Bulimia.* New York: Brunner/Mazel, 1985.

Garfinkel, Paul E. and Garner, David M. *Anorexia Nervosa: A Multidimensional Perspective.* New York: Brunner/Mazel, 1982.

Garner, David M. and Garfinkel, Paul E., eds. *Handbook of Psychotherapy for Anorexia Nervosa and Bulimia.* New York: The Guilford Press, 1985.

Johnson, Craig and Connors, Mary E. *The Etiology and Treatment of Bulimia Nervosa.* New York: Basic Books, 1987.

Kaye, Walter H. and Gwirtsman, Harry E. *A Comprehensive Approach to the Treatment of Normal Weight Bulimia.* Washington, D.C.: A.P.A. Press, 1985.

Minuchin, Salvador et al. *Psychosomatic Families: Anorexia Nervosa in Context.* Cambridge, Mass.: Harvard University Press, 1978.

Schneider, Linda H. et al. *The Psychobiology of Human Eating Disorders: Preclinical and Clinical Perspectives.* New York: The New York Academy of Sciences, 1989.

Strober, Michael, ed. *The International Journal of Eating Disorders.* New York: John Wiley and Sons, 605 Third Avenue, New York, NY 10158. The journal is published six times per year.

Williamson, Donald A. *Assessment of Eating Disorders: Obesity, Anorexia, and Bulimia Nervosa.* New York: Pergamon Press, Inc., 1990.

APPENDIX A
REFERRAL SOURCES

Self-Help Groups
There are several self-help organizations that you can contact at any time. They do not usually offer therapy per se. However, they can refer you to competent professionals in your area and will also assist you in contacting people like yourself who are involved in confronting and combatting eating disorders. These are the addresses of their headquarters. Each can provide you with addresses and phone numbers of local groups in your area.

American Anorexia/Bulimia Association, Inc. (AABA)
418 East 76th Street
New York, NY 10021
212 734-1114
(AABA publishes a newsletter and has chapters throughout the United States.)

Anorexia Nervosa and Related Eating Disorders, Inc. (ANRED)
P.O. Box 5102
Eugene, OR 97405
503 344-1144

Bulimia Anorexia Self-Help, Inc. (BASH)
Deaconess Hospital
6150 Oakland Avenue
St. Louis, MO 63139
314 991-BASH or 800 BAS-HSTL
(BASH also publishes a newsletter.)

Eating Disorders Association
Priory Center
11 Priory Road
High Wycombe, Buckinghamshire HP136SL
England

Eating Disorders Association
Sackville Place
44–48 Magdalen Street
Norwich, Norfolk NR31JE
England

National Association of Anorexia Nervosa and Associated Disorders (ANAD)
P.O. Box 271
Highland Park, IL 60035
312 831-3438

Resources Offering Therapy and Referrals
The following list of resources for people struggling with eating disorders (arranged alphabetically for your convenience) is a sampling of the kind of help available in the United States, Australia, Belgium, Canada, and the United Kingdom. Some are small, private clinics, others are programs affiliated with hospitals and/or universities. The therapies they offer vary.

Inclusion in this list does not constitute an endorsement.

Whether a particular program or therapist is suited to your needs is something you will be able to determine for yourself.

ALABAMA

Center for Eating Disorders, Inc.
2022 Brookwood Medical Center Drive
Suite 404
Birmingham, AL 35209

ARIZONA

Eating Disorders Center of Greater Phoenix
3337 North Miller Road
Suite 105
Scottsdale, AZ 85251
602 994-9773

AUSTRALIA

Eating Disorders Unit
Prince Henry Hospital
Anzac Parade
Little Bay
NSW, 2036
Australia

Eating Disorders Clinic
Prince of Wales Hospital
High Street
Randwick 2031
Sydney, Australia

BELGIUM

Eating Disorders Unit
University Psychiatric Center
Leuvensesteenweg 517
B-3070 Kortenberg,
Belgium

Eating Disorders Program
Brea Hospital Neuropsychiatric Center
875 North Brea Boulevard
Brea, CA 92621
714 529-4963
800 422-4106

Eating Disorder Program
University of California, Irvine
P.O. Box AZ
Irvine, CA 92716
714 856-5414

Adolescent Eating Disorders Program
(also Adult Eating Disorders Clinic)
UCLA Neuropsychiatric Institute
760 Westwood Plaza
Los Angeles, CA 90024

The Association of Eating Disorders Treatment Programs
P.O. Box 6722
Napa, CA 94581

Eating Disorders Program
Children's Hospital at Stanford
520 Sand Hill Road
Palo Alto, CA 94304

Eating Disorders Clinic
Department of Psychiatry
Stanford University School of Medicine
Stanford, CA 94305

CANADA

Eating Disorders Program
Douglas Hospital Center
6875 LaSalle Blvd.

Montreal (Verdun), Quebec H4H 1R3
Canada

The Eating Disorder Center
Toronto General Hospital
200 Elizabeth Street
Toronto, Ontario M5G 2C4
Canada

Eating Disorder Clinic
St. Paul's Hospital
1081 Burrard Street
Vancouver, British Columbia V6Z 1Y9
Canada

Eating Disorders Service
University Hospital — UBC Site
2211 Westbrook Mall
Vancouver, British Columbia V6T 2B5
Canada

Eating Disorders Program
Windsor Western Hospital Centre
Windsor, Ontario
Canada

COLORADO

Eating Disorders Programs
1830 17th Street
Boulder, CO 80302
303 443-5063

CONNECTICUT

Eating Disorder Unit
The Behavioral Medicine Institute
885 Oenoke Ridge Road
New Canaan, CT 06840
203 966-8060

Wilkins Center for Eating Disorders
239 Glenville Road
Greenwich, CT 06830
203 531-1909

Eating Disorder Program
Newington Children's Hospital
Newington, CT 06111
203 667-KIDS

DISTRICT OF COLUMBIA

Eating Disorders Program
Department of Adolescent and Young Adult Medicine
Children's Hospital, National Medical Center
111 Michigan Avenue, NW
Washington, DC 20010

ENGLAND

Eating Disorders Clinic
St. George's Hospital
Cranmer Terrace
London SW17 ORE
England

Anorexia Family Aid National Information Centre
Sackville Place
44 Magdalen Street
Norwich, Norfolk, NR3 1JE
England

FLORIDA

American Anorexia/Bulimia Association of Florida
7900 S.W. 58th Avenue
S. Miami, FL 33143
305 663-1218

ILLINOIS

Eating Disorders Program
Northwestern University Medical School
Institute of Psychiatry, 2nd floor
320 East Huron Street
Chicago, IL 60611

MARYLAND

Eating and Weight Disorders Clinic
The Johns Hopkins Hospital
600 North Wolfe Street
Baltimore, MD 21205

MASSACHUSETTS

Eating Disorders Unit
Department of Psychiatry, ACC 625
Massachusetts General Hospital
15 Parkman Street
Boston, MA 02114

MICHIGAN

Eating Disorders Section
Department of Psychiatry
Michigan State University
B 105 West Fee Hall
Lansing, MI 48824

Department of Psychiatry
University of Michigan Hospitals
1500 East Medical Center Drive
Ann Arbor, MI 48109

MINNESOTA

The Eating Disorders Clinic
University of Minnesota Hospitals
420 Delaware Street, S.E.
Minneapolis, MN 55455

MISSISSIPPI

Eating Disorders Program
Department of Psychiatry and Human Behavior
University of Mississippi Medical Center
2500 North State Street
Jackson, MS 39216-4505

MISSOURI

Eating Disorders Program
St. John's Mercy Medical Center
615 South New Ballas Road
St. Louis, MO 63141

Eating Disorder Services
St. Louis University Medical Center
1221 South Grand Blvd.
St. Louis, MO 63104

NEW JERSEY

Eating Disorders Program
Carrier Foundation
Belle Mead, NJ 08502
908 874-4000

NEW YORK

The Eating Disorder Clinic of the New York State Psychiatric Institute
Columbia Presbyterian Medical Center
723 West 168th Street
New York, NY 10032
212 960-5751

The Center for the Study of Anorexia and Bulimia
1 West 91st Street
New York, NY 10024
212 595-3449

Gracie Square Hospital Eating Disorders Program
420 East 76th Street
New York, NY 10021
Hotline: 212 222-2832
Outside New York: 800 382-2832

The Women's Therapy Center Institute
80 East 11th Street
New York, NY 10003
212 420-1974

Department of Pediatrics, Division of Adolescent Medicine
Montefiore Medical Center
111 East 210th Street
Bronx, NY 10467
212 920-6612

The New York Center for Eating Disorders
490 Third Street
Brooklyn, NY 11215
718 788-6986

American Anorexia/Bulimia Association Westchester Extension Group
White Plains Hospital Medical Center
Davis and East Coast Road
White Plains, NY 10601
914 636-1606

Eating Disorders Program
St. Vincent's Hospital
Harrison, NY 10528

Anorexia Nervosa and Bulimia Nervosa Treatment Program
Cornell Medical Center
New York Hospital, Westchester Division
21 Bloomingdale Road
White Plains, NY 10605

Anorexia/Bulimia Support, Inc.
423 West Onondaga Street
Syracuse, NY 13202
315 428-2241

Adolescent Medical Clinic
University of Rochester Medical Center
Rochester, NY 14627

NORTH CAROLINA

Anorexia Nervosa/Bulimia Treatment Program
Duke University Medical Center
Durham, NC 27710

OHIO

Eating Disorders Clinic
University of Cincinnati Medical College
Cincinnati, OH 45267
513 872-5118

National Anorexic Aid Society
Center for the Treatment of Eating Disorders
5796 Karl Road
Columbus, OH 43229
614 846-2833

PENNSYLVANIA

Philadelphia Child Guidance Clinic
34th and Civic Center Blvd.
Philadelphia, PA 19104
215 387-1919

The Renfrew Center
475 Spring Lane
Philadelphia, PA 19128

The Pittsburgh Educational Network for Eating Disorders, Inc.
(PENED)
P.O. Box 16282
Pittsburgh, PA 15242
412 922-5922

Western Psychiatric Institute and Clinic
University of Pittsburgh
3811 O'Hara Street
Pittsburgh, PA 15213

TEXAS

Eating Disorder Unit
Baylor University Medical Center
3500 Gaston
Dallas, TX 75246
214 820-0111

VIRGINIA

Eating Disorder Program
Dominion Hospital
2960 Sleepy Hollow Road
Falls Church, VA 22044
703 536-2000

American Anorexia/Bulimia Association of Tidewater Virginia, Inc.
P.O. Box 6644
Newport News, VA 23606
804 599-4926

Center for Behavioral Medicine
2819 Parham Road
Richmond, VA 23229

WASHINGTON

The Anorexia Nervosa and Bulimia Resource Center
St. Joseph Hospital
1718 South I Street
Tacoma, WA 98405
206 591-6671

WISCONSIN

Eating Disorders Program
University of Wisconsin Hospital
610 Walnut Street
Madison, WI 53705
608 263-2856

STRAIGHT FACTS
ABOUT NUTRITION

One of the best ways to get a handle on a developing or even a full-blown eating disorder is to educate yourself about nutrition. Ideally, if you're in treatment, one of the people you've been consulting with is a nutritionist, who can help you work out an eating plan that will satisfy you nutritionally *and* emotionally. Just in case you don't have access to such a person yet, and assuming you're willing to face the facts about what you need to eat to stay healthy, the following information is offered to help you get started in the direction of "normal" eating.

The word *calories* refers to energy drawn by the body from the fat cells. A pound of body fat equals 3,500 calories. If you eat more calories than your body needs for daily activity, you gain weight; if you eat fewer calories than your body needs for daily activity, you lose weight. You need calories to live. Different nutrients, though, have different caloric values. Here's a breakdown of the calorie content of these nutrients.

1 gram protein	4 calories
1 gram carbohydrate	4 calories
1 gram fat	9 calories

		Vitamins	0 calories
		Minerals	0 calories
		Water	0 calories

(Source: Boston Children's Hospital with Susan Baker and Roberta R. Henry, *Parents' Guide to Nutrition,* p. 43.)

Males and females have slightly different caloric needs at different times of their lives. There's no such thing as the perfect weight for any one individual (weight depends on one's height, build, activity level, gender, even muscle tone), in spite of the height-weight charts popularized in the past by insurance companies and found in many doctors' offices. It is possible to talk about the number of calories a person needs to consume to maintain a certain weight, and to have an idea of the range of caloric consumption that's considered reasonable to maintain health is useful when trying to figure out what's right for you. The following chart shows the recommended calorie intake for males and females during adolescence and into adulthood.

	Age	Weight (lbs.)	Height (ins.)	Calorie Needs Average/Range
Males	11–14	99	62	2700/2000–3900
	15–18	145	69	2800/2100–3900
	19–22	154	70	2900/2500–3300
	23–50	154	70	2700/2300–3100
Females	11–14	101	62	2200/1500–3000
	15–18	120	64	2100/1200–3000
	19–22	120	64	2100/1700–2500
	23–50	120	64	2000/1600–2400

(Source: Ibid., p. 44.)

Where should you get your calories? According to the Boston Children's Hospital, teenagers generally need more calories than people of any other age. All teenagers need a variety of foods from the four basic food groups — *milk* (or equivalent), *meat, fish, or poultry* (or equivalent), *vegetables and fruits,* and *breads, cereals, and grains* — but are unlikely to eat balanced diets. So, to avoid deficiencies that could negatively affect their health, teenagers need to eat foods rich in calcium like milk and cheeses and vitamin D (to ensure that bones grow properly), iron (to help in the building of muscle mass in boys and to compensate for blood lost in menstruation in girls), B vitamins (because of increased calories eaten), vitamin C (found in citrus fruits), vitamin A (found in yellow or green vegetables or fruits), as well as foods that contain phosphorus and thiamine (Ibid., p. 128). How much should anyone eat (or not eat)? Rather than having to follow a strict diet, it's better to be able to devise your own from within these basic food groups so that your caloric and nutritional requirements are met. It's best — if you're struggling with an eating disorder — to have a doctor or nutritionist help you with this planning at first, but do educate yourself first about your options. See the accompanying table for suggestions.

Basic Four Food Guide for Adolescents
Ages 11–17 Years; (2,100–2,800 calories a day)

Food Group	Recommended Servings Each Day	Average Serving Size
Milk (or equivalent)	4 or more	
Milk, preferably low fat or skim		1 cup
Powdered milk		4 tbsp.
Cheese		1½ oz.
Cottage cheese		1 cup
Yogurt		1 cup

continued

Food Group	Recommended Servings Each Day	Average Serving Size
Meat, fish, poultry (or equivalent)	3 or more	3–5 oz.
Eggs		1–2 whole
Peanut butter		3 tbsp.
Cooked dried peas or beans		1–1½ cups
Luncheon meat		2–3 slices
Vegetables and fruits	4 or more	½–1 cup
Citrus fruits (vitamin C source)	1 or more	
Orange or grapefruit juice		1 cup
Strawberries		1½ cups
Tomatoes or tomato juice		1 cup
Yellow or green vegetable or fruit (vitamin A source)	1 or more	
Broccoli		½ cup
Spinach		½ cup
Carrots		½ cup
Squash		½ cup
Cantaloupe		½ cup
Apricots		8–10 halves
Other fruits and vegetables	2 or more	
Fresh, frozen, canned fruits and vegetables		½ cup
Potato, turnip, most whole vegetables		1 veg.
Apple, banana, most whole fruits		1 fruit
Bread and cereals (whole grain or enriched)	4 or more	
Bread		2 slices
Dry cereal (unsweetened)		1–1½ cups
Cooked cereal, rice, pasta		1 cup or more

(Source: Ibid., p. 129.)

What about Fast Foods?

It's possible to eat fast foods and satisfy some of these nutritional requirements. A hamburger provides the meat-or-equivalent food group, cheese fulfills the milk-and-dairy-product requirement, the bun is the bread-or-cereal representative, lettuce and tomato (minimally) covers the vegetable-and-fruit area, french fries represent the bread-or-cereal (starch) food group, and a milkshake takes care of milk and dairy products once again. This fast-food meal covers the four food groups and includes most essential nutrients (calcium, A and B vitamins, protein, carbohydrate, fat), though it lacks vitamin C, fiber, and folic acid, according to the Boston Children's Hospital.

Fast-food companies provide any interested customer with detailed analyses of the foods they serve in their restaurants. These are updated periodically and can be obtained upon request. For example, McDonald's has a complete ingredient list and nutrition analysis of every item on their menu, available in a pamphlet, "McDonald's Food: The Facts," revised in June 1991. Following are some analyses of fast foods, to give you an idea of what you are and aren't getting if you eat in these kinds of restaurants.

Nutritional Analyses of Fast Foods

	Calories	Protein (gm)	Carbohydrate (gm)	Fat (gm)	Cholesterol (mg)	Sodium (mg)
Arby's						
Roast beef	350	22	32	15	45	880
Beef and cheese	450	27	36	22	55	1220
Super roast beef	620	30	61	28	85	1420
Junior roast beef	220	12	21	9	35	530
Ham and cheese	380	23	33	17	60	1350
Turkey Deluxe	510	28	46	24	70	1220
Club sandwich	560	30	43	30	100	1610

(Source: Consumer Affairs, Arby's Inc., Atlanta, GA. Nutritional analysis by Technological Resources, Camden, NJ.)

	Calories	Protein (gm)	Carbohydrate (gm)	Fat (gm)	Cholesterol (mg)	Sodium (mg)
Dairy Queen						
DQ cone, regular size	230	6	35	7	20	80
DQ dip cone, regular size	300	7	40	13	20	100
DQ sundae, regular size	290	6	51	7	20	120
DQ malt, regular size	600	15	89	20	50	260
DQ float	330	6	59	8	20	85
DQ banana split	540	10	91	15	30	150
DQ parfait	460	10	81	11	30	140
DQ freeze	520	11	89	13	35	180
Mr. Misty freeze	500	10	87	12	35	140
Mr. Misty float	440	6	85	8	20	95

Dilly Bar	240	4	22	15	10	50
DQ sandwich	140	3	24	4	10	40
Mr. Misty Kiss	70	0	17	0	0	tr
Brazier chili dog	330	13	25	20	—	939
Brazier dog	273	11	23	15	—	868
Fish sandwich	400	20	41	17	—	875
Super brazier dog	518	20	41	30	—	1552
Super brazier dog, with cheese	593	26	43	36	—	1986
Brazier fries, small	200	2	25	10	—	115
Brazier onion rings	300	6	33	17	—	140

(Source: International Dairy Queen, Inc., Minneapolis, MN. Nutritional analysis by Raltech Scientific Services, Inc. Madison, WI. Nutritional analysis not applicable in Texas.)

Kentucky Fried Chicken

Original Recipe Dinner*

Wing & rib	603	30	48	32	133	1528
Wing & thigh	661	33	48	38	172	1536
Drumstick & thigh	643	35	46	35	180	1441

Extra Crispy Dinner*

Wing & rib	755	33	60	43	132	1544
Wing & thigh	812	36	58	48	176	1529
Drumstick & thigh	765	38	55	44	183	1480
Mashed potatoes	64	2	12	1	0	268

Nutritional Analyses of Fast Foods (Continued)

	Calories	Protein (gm)	Carbohydrate (gm)	Fat (gm)	Cholesterol (mg)	Sodium (mg)
Gravy	23	0	1	2	0	57
Roll	61	2	11	1	1	118
Corn (5.5″ ear)	169	5	31	3	X	11

*Two pieces chicken, mashed potatoes, gravy, cole slaw, roll.
(Source: Kentucky Fried Chicken, Inc., Louisville, KY. Nutritional analysis by Raltech Scientific Services, Inc., Madison, WI.)

McDonald's

	Calories	Protein (gm)	Carbohydrate (gm)	Fat (gm)	Cholesterol (mg)	Sodium (mg)
Egg McMuffin	327	19	31	15	229	885
English muffin, butter	186	5	30	5	13	318
Hotcakes, butter, syrup	500	8	94	10	47	1070
Sausage (pork)	206	9	tr	19	43	615
Scrambled eggs	180	13	3	13	349	205
Hashbrowns	125	2	14	7	7	325
Big Mac	563	26	41	33	86	1010
Cheeseburger	307	15	30	14	37	767
Hamburger	255	12	30	10	25	520
Quarter Pounder	424	24	33	22	67	735
Quarter Pounder, with cheese	524	30	32	31	96	1236
Filet-O-Fish	432	14	37	25	47	781
French fries, regular size	220	3	26	12	9	109
Apple pie	253	2	29	14	12	398

Cherry pie	260	2	32	14	13	427
McDonaldland cookies	308	4	49	11	10	358
Vanilla shake	352	9	60	8	31	201
Hot fudge sundae	310	7	46	11	18	175
Caramel sundae	328	7	53	10	26	195
Strawberry sundae	289	7	46	9	20	96

(Source: McDonald's Corporation, Oak Brook, IL. Nutritional analysis by Raltech Scientific Services, Inc., Madison, WI.)

Taco Bell

Bean burrito	343	11	48	12	—	272
Beef burrito	466	30	37	21	—	327
Beefy tostada	291	19	21	15	—	138
Bellbeefer	221	15	23	7	—	231
Burrito Supreme	457	21	43	22	—	367
Combination burrito	404	21	43	16	—	300
Enchirito	454	25	42	21	—	1175
Pintos 'N Cheese	168	11	21	5	—	102
Taco	186	15	14	8	—	79
Tostada	179	9	25	6	—	101

(Sources: (1) *Menu Item Portions*, San Antonio, Texas; Taco Bell Co., July 1976. (2) Adams, C.F.: "Nutritive Value of American Foods in Common Units," in *Handbook No. 456.* Washington, D.C.: USDA Agricultural Research Service, November 1975. (3) Church, E.F., Church, H.N. (eds.), *Food Values of Portions Commonly Used*, Twelfth Edition. Philadelphia: J. B. Lippincott Co., 1975. (4) Valley Baptist Medical Center, Food Service Department: *Descriptions of Mexican-American Foods.* Fort Atkinson, WI: NASCO.)

APPENDIX C
A NOTE FROM THE AUTHOR

Whenever you go to a physician or therapist for help in dealing with an eating disorder, it's very important that you inform that person — honestly and accurately — about physical and emotional things that are bothering you. It's possible that the physician or therapist may not ask you about what you want to discuss. It's also possible that a physician or therapist may try to treat you for something other than an eating disorder precisely because the right questions haven't been asked.

Accept the responsibility for representing your problem accurately to the individual who's trying to help you. That is one of the most important things you can do for yourself. For example, if your glands are swollen because you've been vomiting, admit that and don't try to pretend you've just had a bout of the flu. If your menstrual periods have stopped, don't say that you're irregular. If your gums and teeth are affected by bulimic habits, don't try to blame the symptoms on too much candy as a child or poor heredity. If you are taking the major step of getting help for your problem, don't lie about things — ever.

Many health care professionals use a manual called the

DSM-III-R (published by the American Psychiatric Association) to help them correctly diagnose their clients' problems. This is how the *DSM-III-R* describes some of the varieties of eating disorders:

Anorexia Nervosa:
A. Refusal to maintain body weight over a minimal normal weight for age and height, e.g., weight loss leading to maintenance of body weight 15% below that expected; or failure to make expected weight gain during period of growth, leading to body weight 15% below that expected.
B. Intense fear of gaining weight or becoming fat, even though underweight.
C. Disturbance in the way in which one's body weight, size, or shape is experienced, e.g., the person claims to "feel fat" even when emaciated, believes that one area of the body is "too fat" even when obviously underweight.
D. In females, absence of at least three consecutive menstrual cycles when otherwise expected to occur (primary or secondary amenorrhea). (A woman is considered to have amenorrhea if her periods occur only following hormone, e.g., estrogen, administration.)

Bulimia Nervosa:
A. Recurrent episodes of binge eating (rapid consumption of a large amount of food in a discrete period of time).
B. A feeling of lack of control over eating behavior during the eating binges.
C. The person regularly engages in either self-induced vomiting, use of laxatives or diuretics, strict dieting or fasting, or vigorous exercise in order to prevent weight gain.
D. A minimum average of two binge eating episodes a week for at least three months.
E. Persistent overconcern with body shape and weight.

Eating Disorder Not Otherwise Specified: Disorders of eating that do not meet the criteria for a specific Eating Disorder.

Examples:
>   (1) a person of average weight who does not have
>   binge eating episodes, but frequently engages in self-
>   induced vomiting for fear of gaining weight;
>   (2) all of the features of Anorexia Nervosa in a female
>   except absence of menses;
>   (3) all of the features of Bulimia Nervosa except the
>   frequency of binge eating episodes.

It may be easier for you to talk with your therapist about your particular set of problems if you first familiarize yourself with these diagnostic criteria. Then you could say to your therapist, "I think I fit (or don't fit) the *DSM-III-R* definition of _____ (anorexia, bulimia, or an eating disorder not otherwise specified), and here's why I think that. . . . "

Several diagnostic tools in the form of questionnaires are also available to health care professionals and are designed to help therapist and client focus on issues of importance to someone with an eating disorder. These questionnaires (which are also referred to as structured interviews) are typically used as the basis for your first few therapy sessions. Some examples are the Diagnostic Survey for Eating Disorders (DSED), developed in 1984 by Craig Johnson and revised in 1987; the Eating Disorder Examination (EDE), developed by Cooper and Fairburn in 1987 as a way to evaluate bulimia nervosa; and the Interview for Diagnosis of Eating Disorders (IDED), which was described by Donald Williamson (1990) as being used to evaluate anorexia, bulimia, compulsive overeating, and obesity.

These structured interviews are quite detailed and much longer than the self-report checklists (such as the EAT and the BULIT, which you found here in the chapters on anorexia and bulimia). For instance, in one printed version, the DSED is twenty-one pages long. Sometimes a therapist will ask a new client to actually write out the answers to the questions in one of these structured interviews by filling out a preprinted form; sometimes a therapist will ask the questions in a conversational way.

No matter how your therapist presents the material to you, be prepared to answer a lot of questions, maybe more than you really want to answer, especialy the first time you meet. But don't be put off by the experience. The first interview is very important, and whether the DSED or some other question-and-answer format is used as a starting point, expect to be asked about your weight history; your attitudes about weight; how your body is proportioned; dieting behavior; binge eating behavior; purging behavior (and how you feel before and after bingeing and purging); your exercise regimen; other behavior such as smoking and alcohol and drug use; a sexual history; a menstrual history (if you're female); and a medical and psychiatric history (including information about any medications you've taken or are taking, prior hospitalizations, and prior therapies). In addition, a family history and how you rate your relationships with various people in your life are often included.

Although some people are initially intimidated by having to think about and answer such a barrage of questions, most will admit that after the shock of having to face all this wears off, the experience of responding to such a questionnaire is clearly positive. Why? It helps them focus on what has really been bothering them, helps them see inconsistencies between what they *thought* they'd been accomplishing by holding on to an eating disorder and what had *actually* been happening as a result of their anorexia and/or bulimia, and, by giving them some sense of direction, helps them find the courage to begin to challenge an eating-disordered way of life.

A physician or therapist who's knowledgeable about working with anorectics and bulimics will explore such topics with you as an integral part of your therapy. If you are now seeing someone who isn't doing this, you might ask about the possibility of discussing such topics. If the therapist refuses, you might decide it's time to seek help from someone who won't refuse.